# How to
# RESTORE
## Your
# FARM TRACTOR

04-2392

Robert N. Pripps

*Motorbooks International*
Publishers & Wholesalers ®

*To Greg, my number-two son
and a good tractor mechanic*

First published in 1992 by Motorbooks International
Publishers & Wholesalers, PO Box 2, 729 Prospect
Avenue, Osceola, WI 54020 USA

Motorbooks International is a certified trademark,
registered with the United States Patent Office

The information in this book is true and complete to the
best of our knowledge. All recommendations are made
without any guarantee on the part of the author or
Publisher, who also disclaim any liability incurred in
connection with the use of this data or specific details

Motorbooks International recommends you follow all
safety procedures when working on your vehicle. Wear
eye protection and a respiration filter, especially when
painting and around tools. Always dispose of hazardous
fluids, batteries, tires and parts properly and safely to
protect our environment

We recognize that some words, model names and
designations, for example, mentioned herein are the
property of the trademark holder. We use them for
identification purposes only. This is not an offical
publication

Motorbooks International books are also available at
discounts in bulk quantity for industrial or sales-
promotional use. For details write to Special Sales
Manager at the Publisher's address

Library of Congress Cataloging-in-Publication Data

Pripps, Robert N.
    How to restore your farm tractor / Robert N. Pripps.
       p.   cm.
    Includes index.
    ISBN 0-87938-593-6
    1.  Farm tractors—Maintenance and repair—
       Amateurs' manuals.
  I.  Title.
TL233.2.P75 1992
629.28'75—dc20                    91-40770

**On the front cover:** *The Farmall A restored as a project
covered in this book. Restoration work was done by Joe
Schloskey's Machinery Hill of Phillips, Wisconsin.*
Andrew Morland

**On the back cover:** *The Ford-Ferguson 9N tractor, serial
number 357, restored as a project covered in this book.
Restoration work was done by Palmer Fossum of
Northfield, Minnesota.* Andrew Morland

Printed and bound in the United States of America

# Contents

# Acknowledgments

Many people, organizations and companies helped me write this book—some without knowing it. Without their help, I could not have completed it. I would like to gratefully acknowledge the contributions of some who were especially helpful:

Intertec Publishing Corporation and Editorial Director Randy Stephens, for providing fifty pieces of artwork from their tractor service manuals and for manuals and other technical publications for use as references. Intertec tractor service manuals are sold under the title of *I&T Shop Service Manual* and are available for most popular tractor makes and models.

Dr. Buryl McFadden, Air Force engine scientist, farmer and tractor collector, for providing technical advice and assistance.

Donna Hull, and the American Society of Agricultural Engineers, for providing several pieces of artwork from their great books, *The Agricultural Tractor 1855-1950* by R. B. Gray, and *Farm Tractors 1950-1975* by Lester Larsen.

These books are available from Motorbooks International Publishers & Wholesalers, P.O. Box 2, 729 Prospect Avenue, Osceola, WI 54020 USA.

Paul Hesterberg, raconteur of tractor lore and an old tractor buff, for many insights into tractor history.

Palmer Fossum and Joe Schloskey, restorers of the project tractors done for this book, for their help with the photography and patience in answering questions.

Deere and Company, Moline, Illinois, especially Lori Lees and Ralph Hughes, for their help with pictures and for their technical advice.

Ford-New Holland, New Holland, Pennsylvania, and Public Affairs Director Mark Bransetter, for providing on-going help, pictures and manuals.

Artistic Photo Lab, Inc., Rockford, Illinois, for special care in developing the photos used in this book.

Final thanks to Dave Mowitz, senior machinery editor at *Successful Farming* magazine, for his sharing of club addresses and parts sources that help make up the appendices.

# Introduction

Do you need a new tractor, but have found the price mindboggling? Do you have a large area to mow—too much for a "riding mower," but not enough to justify a new mowing tractor? Do you have some property in the country, and would like some help with the gardening, grading, snow removal and firewood gathering? Or maybe someplace in your memory there is a warm spot for a particular brand of old tractor; perhaps you learned to drive on one, or perhaps your dad or granddad had one. Or are you handy with tools and looking for a way to make some money?

Any or all of the above reasons (or excuses) make you a candidate for the fun and profit of restoring old tractors.

There are two basic approaches to restoring an old tractor—as a hobby or for business. And there are two basic ways to restore an old tractor—as a show tractor or as a work tractor. Ideally, your hobby could be your business, and you could restore work tractors to show condition. The main difference in approaches is whether you want "original configuration." In a work tractor, such things as a twelve-volt electrical system conversion or modern-tread tires

*A show-quality John Deere Model A. Close examination reveals a tire tread pattern of a more modern era, however.*

*A nice pair of restored Farmalls, a 300 and a C, ready for a parade or work in the field.*

might be a real advantage and an improvement. But, these things are to be avoided in a show tractor.

There are also variations in the degree to which you may want to go with either type of tractor. Some individuals merely get old tractors that don't run, paint them and set them in their front yards as conversation pieces. Others go so far in the restoration process that their tractors are actually far better than when they rolled off the showroom floors. Each old tractor represents an important achievement in the history of mechanics, so no matter why you want to undertake a restoration or to what lengths you are willing to go to achieve accurate originality, you will be well rewarded in satisfaction for your efforts.

Old tractor restoration is one of the fastest-growing hobbies among farmers. Many have an "old beater" around the place, with many fond memories attached to it. They usually also have the space, tools and know-how to complete a restoration. In addition, the winter months often afford some respite from crop production, allowing time for hobbies.

As the price of new tractors goes up, more and more handy individuals are finding an opportunity to make a profit in rejuvenating work tractors for sale. Some individuals do as many as twelve per year, usually concentrating on one or two brands. Others, such as Joe Schloskey (who you will meet a little later), rebuild work tractors as a fill-in for slack time in their regular businesses.

Where do you fit? You probably want to know what is required in tools, space and talent. You are also perhaps just a little curious about costs: what to pay for a junker, how much restoration will cost and how much the tractor will be worth when you're done. This book, then, is for you: men and women who like old tractors and are interested in restoring and preserving them. We will look into all facets of fixing up old tractors and, together with two experienced restorers, we will follow in text and pictures the work done on two tractors: one to be restored to original condition for show purposes, and the other for resale as a work tractor.

So, come on, get on your work clothes and let's head for the shop!

# Chapter 1

# Choosing Your Tractor

First of all, you must be realistic. You may have a lead on a Huber 40/20 Steamer, stored for fifty years in someone's barn, but that doesn't mean it would make a good first restoration project for a neophyte. Obviously, getting an old orphan tractor restored is going to be more difficult than restoring one whose manufacturer is still in the tractor business. But the degree of difficulty is not your first consideration; your first consideration must be not "what," but "why?"

If your motivation is strictly nostalgia, perhaps for your favorite childhood machine, then by all means go for it. You won't be satisfied with anything less. This may mean, however, tackling an easier job first to gain experience. You must also decide whether you want to restore a tractor for work or whether you want a parade item, original in every respect.

**Which Tractor to Restore?**

Once you've settled the "why" criteria, you can begin homing in on the make and model that is right for you. Remember, knowledge is going to be your greatest asset in selecting a good value, so get some materials on old tractors; get the *I&T Shop Service Manual* and the Nebraska Tractor Test Data for the

*January in Minnesota as Palmer Fossum and Ken Moravec roll the Ford-Ferguson 9N serial number 357 into the shop to prepare it for a complete show-quality restoration.*

*Talk about restored to showroom condition! This 1937 John Deere Model G General Purpose tractor resides in the showroom of the headquarters of Deere and Company, Moline, Illinois.*

one you're most interested in, for example. Ask questions of people who know about the type, and if there is a club or newsletter associated with the brand, subscribe (see the Sources appendix for addresses).

If your purpose in undertaking the restoration is to make a profit, your tractor choice is narrowed considerably. You must buy one that will fill a need when completed so you can sell it again. The 15 to 30 horsepower wide-front machines for mowing and landscaping will probably find the most available market. Beware of tractors with fewer than 15 horsepower, as they are generally inadequate for serious work. Wide-front tractors with 30 to 50 horsepower and with front-end loaders will also be in quite good demand. Those with narrow fronts or those without hydraulics will be at somewhat of a disadvantage in today's market, regardless of the horsepower.

One factor that you must consider in choosing a tractor for restoration is cost. For as in the Biblical

*A nicely restored 1942 Case SC pulls a McCormick PTO binder at the 1991 Franklin Grove, Illinois, thresheree. Large amounts of bound grain bundles are consumed by* the old-time threshers at these events all over the US and Canada.

admonition: " . . . which of you, intending to build a tower, sitteth not down first, and counteth the cost, whether he have sufficient to finish it?" (Luke 14:28)

When considering how much you'll have to pay for your dream tractor and how much it will cost to fix it up, remember that if the tractor was expensive when it was new, it most likely still is. This alone should not deter you, as the finished product should be worth the costs. If you are of modest means, and would not normally spend money on "luxury" items, you would be wise to use discretion at this point. Perhaps a Massey Pony would be better for you than that John Deere R you've had your eye on.

One rule of thumb for estimating what an old tractor will cost today is: If it is in average working condition, if it is not rare or of a limited-production run or if it is not so old that its antique nature inflates its value, it should cost today somewhere around what it cost new. This should give you a starting point.

## Finding Tractors

Where do you find a particular tractor model or type? The first place to look is in the classified section of your local newspaper. If what you want is somewhat rarer than a Farmall M, you might consider placing an ad yourself. The advantage of finding what you want locally cannot be overstated. Once you've driven 300 miles with your trailer, your analysis of the tractor can sometimes be less objective than if it was in your own backyard.

Failing to find a tractor close to home, the next place to turn is the club or newsletter for the particular brand you are seeking. The club secretary or newsletter editor will likely have a listing of tractors for sale, and if what you seek does not pop up, get the names of folks who have that model, even though not for sale. They may know of others who either have one for sale or know of one elsewhere.

So now, before we get into the details, let us take a closer look into the pros and cons of show versus work restoration. We'll meet some tractor restorers and some tractors to be restored.

## Restoring a Show Tractor

To illustrate the process of restoring a tractor to original condition for use in parades and as an

*The 9N's serial number. Palmer Fossum almost missed the significance of this tractor, because so many of its identifying characteristics had been altered over the years—until he saw this number. Serial number 357 is one of only 10,233 Ford-Fergusons made in 1939. It was probably made in the first week of production.*

*Ford-Ferguson 9N serial number 357 as Fossum found it. So many things had been changed and updated over the tractor's past fifty-one years of labor that it looked more like the later 2N model than the historic 9N it is.*

*The thing that caught Palmer Fossum's eye on the 9N, indicating an antique worth further investigation, was the left brake pedal. The earliest of Ford-Ferguson 9N tractors had interchangeable (reversible) left and right brake pedals. It pays to know your tractor history and parts details.*

historic show piece, we will follow throughout this book a 1939 Ford-Ferguson 9N, serial number 357, owned and restored by Palmer Fossum of Northfield, Minnesota.

We chose the 9N for three reasons. First, not only was the 9N one of the most popular tractors ever built, it was also a pivotal tractor in agricultural history. This was the first tractor with a three-point hitch—the Ferguson System of integrated implements, hydraulically lifted and with automatic depth control—to be mass produced. Before the 9N, tractors pulled their implements in much the same way as a horse did, attached by a short length of chain or a cleavis and a pin. In some cases, another operator was required to control the implement; in others, the tractor driver (seated as far aft as possible) could reach back and control the implement. With the Ford-Ferguson, the operator (seated in front of the rear axle) manipulated the implement with a hydraulic control lever beside his seat.

Not only was this much easier for the operator, but the System also automatically adjusted the implement for changing soil conditions by raising or lowering it to maintain a constant draft, or pull. Also, as draft increased and the System began to raise the implement, the downforce on the rear tires increased, improving traction.

The System also improved safety. On earlier tractors, when a trailing implement, such as a plow, encountered a buried rock or other obstruction, the tractor tended to flip over backwards. The Ferguson System eliminated that tendency. Harry Ferguson's System was so good that as soon as the patents for the three-point hitch ran out (or could be circumvented), all tractor manufacturers introduced their own versions.

Second, the 9N, especially serial number 357, represents an interesting degree of complexity for the restorer as it was an extremely early 9N tractor, the 357th built. To put serial number 357 into first-class working condition for resale to a landscaper would not present much of a challenge because virtually all parts are stock catalog items. But to put serial number 357 into original condition would require a wide

*The collection of hard-to-find parts that Palmer Fossum assembled prior to beginning the restoration of Ford-Ferguson 9N serial number 357.*

*The Farmall A was taken from Machinery Hill's "bone yard" before being maneuvered into the shop to begin the work tractor renovation. Machinery Hill owner Joe Schloskey bought the little tractor sight unseen, over the telephone, and was somewhat dismayed at its appearance when he finally saw it. Nevertheless, it turned out to be in fairly good mechanical condition.*

*Pushing the Farmall A into the shop at Machinery Hill to start work. Note the 1940 Ford-Ferguson 9N being used to push the Farmall A. "Nothing fancy," says Joe Schloskey, "but it's been on duty here for many years."*

variety of scrounging techniques, and would show the lengths to which restorers must be willing to go in pursuit of correctness.

Third, the 9N is fairly small and lightweight and would not require heavy equipment or an inordinate amount of space to work on it.

Palmer Fossum is a retired dairy farmer. He is quite familiar with Ford tractors; he owns almost sixty of them, the earliest being a 1924 Fordson and the latest being a 1959 Ford 981. Several years ago, Fossum decided to sell his cows and turn his tractor collecting into a full-time business. He, and his one employee, Ken Moravec, are in charge of restorations.

He hasn't regretted that decision.

The business keeps him traveling to auctions and sales, looking for collectible tractors, parts and old advertisements and sales literature. When not out looking, Fossum keeps extremely busy at his place in Northfield getting parts for customers, answering phone calls from people looking for a particular item and working on his own restorations.

Fossum is not only an expert on finding rare parts, he is an expert on knowing what parts should be on each Ford tractor year model. He remembers going with his father in 1940 to pick up a new Ford 9N, trading in a 1924 Fordson. From that time on, he began collecting and filing away in his memory details of each model change. As an interesting aside, Fossum remembers that the dealer delivered the 9N

on an extremely cold winter day, expecting to find a loading dock or ramp of some kind to use to get the tractor off the truck. There was no such thing in the neighborhood; they finally hit upon the idea of backing the truck up to a frozen manure pile. Thus, the little Ford made a rather ignominious entrance to the farm it would serve for the next ten years.

Fossum took serial number 357 in on trade from a man who bought from him a 1954 Ford Golden Jubilee tractor, allowing him $850. Fossum had tried to buy serial number 357 several years earlier at a farm sale, but when the bidding passed $1,100, he dropped out. He then told the successful bidder to let him know if he ever wanted to sell it. After serial number 357 had done routine farm chores for the man for about six years, he decided to upgrade to the Jubilee, and called Fossum.

When Fossum had first seen serial number 357 at the farm sale, he had nearly passed it up because of its appearance. Almost all evidence of its historic significance had been removed and replaced over the fifty years of its working life. It had later-model fenders, hood, grille, steering wheel, instrument panel, axles, radiator and radiator cap, front and rear tires, generator, sediment bowl, fan and seat. To return serial number 357 to original condition would challenge even Palmer Fossum's scrounging ability.

Probably the most difficult item for him to find was the correct hood. The first 700-800 9N Ford tractors were delivered with cast aluminum hoods, which, of course, includes serial number 357. That means that any tractor with an aluminum hood is, in its own right, a significant collectible.

Fossum was able to determine what happened to the original hood that came with serial number 357. The widow of the original owner, the one who had the farm sale at which Fossum had bid on the tractor, told him that a tree had fallen on the tractor early in its life, shattering the hood. The hood had been replaced with one made of steel of the type then being used on 9Ns. The widow told Fossum that the broken pieces had been thrown on a junk pile in a gully on an unused section of the farm. Fossum found pieces of the hood in the trash heap, but not enough of it to have it repaired. Thus, a search was immediately begun for the correct aluminum hood in order to bring serial number 357 back to its original configuration.

## Restoring a Work Tractor

We will also follow the rejuvenation of a work tractor: a Farmall A, owned by Joe Schloskey. Schloskey's business, Machinery Hill, is located on a hill south of the town of Phillips, in northern Wisconsin.

We chose the Farmall A because it is in the center of a broad spectrum of small tractors made by several manufacturers that are of interest to restorers for both work and show. These include several models by John Deere and Allis Chalmers and the Farmall A, B, C and Cub. These are excellent utility tractors for light-duty tasks, such as lawn mowing, cultivating, gathering firewood and sawing cordwood by using the power takeoff.

Both the Farmall A and Ford-Ferguson 9N were introduced in 1939. The Farmall was produced without much variation as the A and Super A (with hydraulics) through 1954. From then until 1979, the same basic tractor, with cosmetic changes, was offered as the Model 100, 130 and 140—a forty-year production run.

The big feature when the A was introduced was Culti-Vision, the tradename for a new design, offsetting the engine to the left and the driver seat to the right. This gave the driver an unobstructed view of the operation of a belly-mounted cultivator. Arranging the engine like this meant that a weighted right rear wheel could be installed so that the tractor wouldn't roll over when making sharp right turns.

The Farmall AV was an adaptation of the basic A for high-clearance applications, such as asparagus cultivation; it provided an extra 6in. of crop clearance. The Farmall B is essentially the same tractor as the A, but with a narrow front end.

*Machinery Hill mechanic Roger Wywialowski begins the teardown of the Farmall A. The fluids have been drained and the hood removed, and Wywialowski is in the process of pulling the radiator.*

Like the Ford-Ferguson, the Farmall A makes a good project because it is light in weight and small and its restoration does not require special skill or equipment.

When restored as a work tractor, the Farmall would be equipped with a Woods mower deck. This is an advantage over the Ford-Ferguson: It is much easier to mount a mower under the belly of a Farmall A because of the clearance. Belly mowers do a better job on lawns than do rear-mounted mowers and are much easier to operate in tight quarters.

This Farmall A should sell quite readily for around $3,000. A new mowing tractor with the same power range would be a much-less-substantial, one- or two-cylinder, air-cooled type that would cost almost twice that much. Besides, the Farmall A looks rather like a scale model of the giant Farmall M, and an operator feels much more significant on one of them than on a "garden tractor." Let's face it, it brings out the Walter Mitty in all of us!

Schloskey is a relatively young man for owning a business requiring such a broad spectrum of experience. His grandfather founded the business back when machine farming was in its infancy. Joe's grandfather was a cattle hauler, taking livestock from northern Wisconsin to the markets down-state and in Chicago. When the farmers he was hauling for realized that his large cattle truck was coming back empty, they began asking him to haul back pieces of machinery that were not available in the north. As time went on, he recognized the opportunity to pick up additional machinery on speculation, and eventually he had no more time for the cattle business.

Joe's father took over the business in 1958, when Grandfather lost his life in an unfortunate drowning accident. Joe's dad operated the business, with young Joe as an apprentice, until he retired in 1985. He had moved into the used tractor parts business by accident. In the early sixties, he bought a tractor for resale, but later found that it had a cracked block. Since he couldn't sell it as it was, he parked it out in back. Soon, customers inquired about removing parts. When the tractor was almost gone, Joe's father realized that he had made more on it than if he'd sold it in one piece.

Joe was twenty-eight when he took over and further developed the business into one specializing in heavy-duty earth-moving and logging equipment while still handling farm, construction and estate tractors. Now, there is a substantial farm tractor

graveyard out in back, providing a large variety of parts for Joe's use or for sale to restorers.

The Farmall A made its home in this graveyard for several years after he bought it over the phone, sight unseen, for $500. Schloskey admits he was a little dismayed at its condition when he went to pick it up.

Schloskey has found that being a dealer for Woods equipment helps draw customers—they are interested in purchasing a mower deck if he has a nice-looking small tractor with such a deck in the front row of his lot, and this was the reason he purchased the Farmall A. This particular Farmall A has a starter (many do not) and a distributor ignition (many have magneto ignition systems).

Machinery Hill usually employs three or four mechanics, with Schloskey ordering parts, selling and sometimes helping out with a wrench. Roger Wywialowski did the teardown of the Farmall A, and Tom Marsh did the rebuilding and re-assembly.

*Joe Schloskey, owner of Machinery Hill, Phillips, Wisconsin. Schloskey took over the business when his father retired in 1985. He was twenty-seven at the time. The Farmall A is dwarfed by its stablemates, some giant*

*logging equipment such as the John Deere 440 Skidder in the background. Rebuilding and sale of such logging and construction equipment is the backbone of Machinery Hill's business.*

Instrumentation was not the long suit of the Farmall A. Only an ammeter is provided. The knob below is the manual voltage regulator: one position for normal running, the second for operation with the lights on.

Another way to be a tractor collector: models. This example of a model Ford Golden Jubilee is owned by Donna Wernberg of Rockford, Illinois. It was sold to her father along with a new full-size Jubilee back in 1953. Many tractor restorers try to collect scale models of their rebuilt tractors.

# Chapter 2

# Buying Your Tractor

Acquiring a tractor for restoration can be an exciting experience, especially if you had to search diligently for the particular antique you had in mind. Or, it can be as mundane as Joe Schloskey picking up the phone and offering the owner of the Farmall A $500 for it. For most of us, a quick phone deal is not recommended; even if we have a work tractor in mind, we should approach the purchase in an orderly and deliberate fashion. (Schloskey will be quick to tell you that he buys very few tractors over the phone.)

**Checklist**

The checklist included in this chapter will help you organize your thoughts and will help you decide how much to offer for a tractor. When faced with more than one choice, some find it helpful to "weigh" checklist items (see examples) according to their importance. Weightings are, of course, subjective. You would do well to have in mind the items to be heavily weighted before you get too involved with a particular tractor.

*A set of John Deere Regular or Wheatland tractors. In the foreground is a Model BR with a Model D in the back-* *ground. Many collectors strive to complete a series of matching tractor types.*

If it is your intention to sell the tractor when finished, the weighting factors will reflect anticipated costs. If you are restoring a show tractor to keep, your weightings will reflect areas of difficulty.

When considering the purchase of a tractor far away from you, get as much information about its condition as you can before making the trip. You might consider sending the checklist to the owner and asking him to fill it out and return it, along with some pictures. Even with precautions, however, don't be surprised if things are not all that you expected.

Automobile restorers have come up with some generally accepted classes to describe a car's condition. Tractor buffs are beginning to adopt these same classifications.

Class 1, Excellent: Restored to current professional standards in every area, or completely original. All components operating. In all appearances, brand new.

Class 2, Fine: Well restored, or a superior restoration along with excellent original; or extremely well-maintained original showing minimal wear.

Class 3, Very Good: Completely operable original; an older restoration now showing wear; an amateur restoration. Presentable and serviceable

### Weighted Rating Tables: Ford-Ferguson 9N, Serial Number 357

| Item to Consider | Rating (On a Scale of 1 to 10) | Weighting Factor | Total Points |
|---|---|---|---|
| General Appearance | 7 | 200 | 1400 |
| Steering System | 5 | 100 | 500 |
| Engine | 5 | 100 | 500 |
| Electrical System | 6 | 50 | 300 |
| Clutch/Transmission | 7 | 100 | 700 |
| Rear Axle | 4 | 50 | 200 |
| Hydraulic System | 8 | 100 | 800 |
| Brakes | 6 | 150 | 900 |
| Total Points (out of a possible 8500) | | | 5300 |

*Alvin White of Kingston, Illinois, owns this 1949 John Deere MT. While it is in virtual show condition, it does routine work around the farm, including pulling the tank trailer, as shown. White also has a three-point plow and cultivator for the MT.*

## Weighted Rating Table: Farmall A

| Item to Consider | Rating (On a Scale of 1 to 10) | Weighting Factor | Total Points |
|---|---|---|---|
| General Appearance | 5 | 200 | 1000 |
| Steering System | 3 | 100 | 300 |
| Engine | 5 | 100 | 500 |
| Electrical System | 2 | 50 | 100 |
| Clutch/Transmission | 6 | 100 | 600 |
| Rear Axle | 8 | 50 | 400 |
| Hydraulic System | 0 | 100 | 0 |
| Brakes | 4 | 150 | 600 |
| Total Points (out of a possible 8500) | | | 3500 |

inside and out, but not a Class 1 or 2. Also in this class are good partial restorations with parts to complete, and other variations on the theme.

Class 4, Good: Operable, or needing minor work to become operable. A deteriorated or poorly

*A yard guard. It's obvious from the grass beneath this Farmall that it hasn't moved for quite a while, nor has the mannequin at the wheel. This is one end of the restoration scale—just a good paint job and some new decals.*

accomplished restoration. In need of complete restoration, but mostly usable as is.

Class 5, Restorable: Needs complete restoration. Not drivable, but not weathered, wrecked or stripped to the point of being useful only for salvage.

When work on them began, our Farmall A was a Class 5, and the Ford-Ferguson was a Class 4.

The numbers in the Rating column reflect the relative value of the various items; a scale of one to ten was chosen, but use whatever works for you. The Weighting Factor numbers reflect the relative importance of each item. For example, you could include for General Appearance such things as uniqueness or appropriateness for the anticipated task.

These weightings and ratings are subjective, of course. Someone else would have come up with different numbers than those shown on the examples. There are ways to further systematize the ratings by assigning points for factors, which, if all are good, will total ten. For example, if there are ten inspection points in the steering mechanism, you could assign one point for each that did not need repair.

The real purpose in a weighted rating is not to quantify things to the point of eliminating subjectivity, but to control the subjectivity so that it is as consistent as possible when examining several competing tractors. For example, if you were trying to decide which of the two, the Farmall A or the Ford-Ferguson, was the best buy, you could divide the total points by the selling price, and compare the quotients:

$$\text{Farmall A } \frac{3500}{500} = 7$$

$$\text{Ford-Ferguson } \frac{5300}{850} = 6.3$$

This would tell you that the Ford-Ferguson, at $850, is not quite as good a value for the dollar as the

Farmall A, at $500. An equivalent price for the Ford-Ferguson would have been around $750.

Now, you have exact numbers to justify that, which at best, is not very scientific. Don't get too carried away with quantifying the ratings.

## Tractor Purchase Checklist

Unless the tractor has been run recently, you should conduct these tests before attempting to start the engine. Not only will this prevent damage from such things as lack of oil, but it will also allow you to check for water in the oil, or oil in the water, before the fluids get mixed up. It will also serve as a set-up checklist, so that you don't, for example, attempt to start the engine with the fuel shut off.

## General Appearance
- Sheet metal, grille, fenders
- Tires, wheels
- Steering wheel
- Exhaust system
- Oil, water or fuel leaks
- Model designation
- Serial number

*A 1939 John Deere Model B owned by Chuck Daringer of Belvidere, Illinois, who uses it regularly with a disc, harrow and cultipactor.*

*This old McCormick sets under a tree awaiting the loving touch of a restorer.*

Except for the model designation and serial number, these items are self-explanatory. These are included so that proper credit will be given if the tractor is historically significant or rare. Also, if the model designation and serial number are not known, it may be difficult to obtain parts.

## Steering System
- Steering wheel free play
- King pin free play
- Radius rod free play
- Front wheel bearing free play
- Drag arm(s) free play

Steering wheel free play of 2 in., measured at the rim, is about the limit of acceptability. See the chapter on front axles and steering systems for other details.

## Engine
- Evidence of crack repair in block or head
- Oil in crankcase

- Filter(s) in place
- Water in radiator
- Oil in water
- Belts
- Hoses
- Radiator cap
- Air cleaner
- Carburetor controls
- Fuel in tank
- Fuel filter: sediment bowl, shut-off

As you check off these items, get the engine ready to start; that is, open the fuel shut-off, add oil as necessary and so on. If the engine is inoperable, this sequence is not as important.

## Electrical System
- Battery: securely in place, overall condition, enough water
- Cables and terminals
- Generator and brushes
- Starter: visible condition

*The unique Allis-Chalmers Model G rear-engine tractor. This nicely restored 1949 model is ready for a summer's mowing.*

*This 1956 Ford Model 860 makes a great work tractor, with a 40 hp engine, five-speed transmission, live hydraulics and PTO.*

*The 1948 Allis-Chalmers WD featured live hydraulics and PTO. The straight-frame channels allow conversion to a wide-front end.*

- Key and switch: location, operation
- Ammeter indication: key on and off
- Plug wire condition
- General wiring condition
- Lights

The ammeter indication item is intended to show that the ignition system and switch are functional by observing an indication of discharge on the ammeter when the switch is turned on. It should be noted, however, that some ammeters are not sensitive enough to show this indication.

## Clutch and Transmission
- Clutch pedal operation
- Shift lever operation
- Oil level
- Water in oil
- Leaks, welds or repairs

It is important to ascertain that the clutch pedal actually releases the clutch and that the shift lever actually moves the gears, especially if there is no starter neutral safety interlock. Occasionally, if the tractor is stored outside, rain will collect in the transmission, so check for water on the dipstick. In cold weather, this water may freeze, preventing clutch or gearshift operation.

## Rear Axle
- Correct operation
- Housing cracks, repairs or leaks
- Lubricant level: water present?
- Axle wheel seals
- Brakes: lining and linkage
- PTO leaks

The correct operation item helps determine that when the drive wheels are off the ground, operating one wheel by hand, the other wheel rotates in the opposite direction.

## Hydraulic System
- Roll test
- Leaks

*One of the niftiest little tractors ever made, this 1945 John Deere LA boasted a 13 hp, two-cylinder engine. These were* *excellent tractors for flat belt powering devices such as choppers and shellers.*

*The Cockshutt, shown here, as well as the Massey-Harris-Ferguson tractors are Canadian-built, and are especially popular with Canadian collectors. This 1958 Model 550*

*Diesel, however, is owned by an Illinois enthusiast. The 550 uses a Hercules four-cylinder engine.*

*The late, styled AR was produced from 1949 into 1953. These are quite rare, and are popular with collectors.*

A hydraulic roll test is a means of ascertaining the functionality of a non-live system without the engine running. This is done by putting the valve in the raise position and rolling the tractor forward in neutral. If the system is functional, the lift should come up. If the engine is operable, this test is not necessary, as the lift can be tested later, after it is started.

After checking all of these items with the engine off, start the tractor and continue your checklist.

## Engine
- Oil pressure
- Smoke from tailpipe, breather

- Knocking or missing
- Temperature stabilizes
- Throttle response: rpm range and governor operation
- Oil and water leaks
- Starter operation
- Generator charging

See the chapter on engines for details on how to test the governor.

## Clutch and Transmission
- Clutch releases completely
- Gear selection
- Clutch engages smoothly
- Clutch slippage
- Free pedal
- PTO operation

The amount of clutch "free pedal" allowable can be found in the *I&T Shop Service Manual* or the owner's manual.

## Hydraulic System
- Lift ability
- Leaks
- Leakdown
- Smoothness

*By the late fifties, tractor instrumentation was becoming much more complete. This Ford panel includes fuel quantity, coolant temperature, engine oil pressure and a time-recording tachometer.*

*A 1925 Fordson parked at a restaurant along the Alcan Highway near Tok, Alaska. The tractor was delivered to a gold mine when new for use in providing flat belt power. The gold became uneconomical to mine soon after, so the tractor was abandoned along with the mine. In 1989, the sons of the restaurant owner, who are bush pilots, dismantled the tractor and flew it out as parts, later to reassemble it as an almost-new Fordson.*

- Draft control
- Position control

Lift ability depends on the size of the tractor; a Ford-Ferguson, or similar size tractor, should be able to lift at least 700 lb. at the three-point uniballs. Draft control and position control are checked in the road-field test. Here, you are merely checking the controls for operation. See the chapter on hydraulic systems for a description of these items.

## Road-Field Test
- Steering shimmy and binding
- Brakes power: left and right
- Engine operation under load
- Governor performance
- Hydraulics operation
- Water temperature
- Inappropriate noises

Ideally, you will be able to test the tractor in a field with an implement, such as a plow. If that isn't possible, you'll have to be content with just driving it around. Try all the gears. Operate it long enough for things to get warm. Test criteria are described in other chapters.

## Bargaining, Paying, Bill of Sale
It is best to have a price in mind when you first contact the prospective seller, but the seller should quote his asking price first. The same is true of auctions: Have your upper-limit dollar figure firmly in mind before the bidding starts. With an individual seller, you usually start at his price and bargain downward; with the auction, the opposite is true. If you find you are too far apart, explain to the seller how you arrived at your figure (based on similar sales, advertisements or estimated value upon completion) and then give him your name and phone number (written down, so he won't have to rely on just his memory) and leave.

If your facts are accurate and your argument convincing, he may come around, but you probably won't convince him to drastically lower his price.

*A fine example of what to look for in a collector tractor, this 1939 Cletrac General GG lies derelict in a field along the road. It comes equipped with a mounted cultivator. Avery later took over this design.*

Don't overlook the opportunity for bartering in the transaction. Perhaps you have something to trade or can provide some kind of professional service for the seller, or maybe there are things that can be "thrown in" on the deal. For example, the seller may be in a position to transport the tractor home for you, or you may require that he do some work on it before you take it away.

Once you've struck a deal, you'll be expected to come up with an acceptable form of payment (assuming it wasn't a complete barter deal). If you are close to home, matters are simplified: Write a check for the amount, wait for the check to clear and then pick up your tractor. If waiting is not acceptable or if the seller requests, you'll need cash, a certified check or travelers checks. Unless you have already agreed on a price, the certified check will likely not be for the right amount. Make it out for the amount of your initial offer and then add to it with cash or travelers checks to bring the amount up to the final, agreed-upon price. If the amount of the transaction is small,

or if the difference between the cashier's check and the final price is not too great, some sellers may accept a personal check, but you should determine that early on.

Tractors are unlike automobiles in that they do not have officially registered titles. How do you know, or how can you find out, whether the person you are bargaining with really owns the tractor he is trying to sell you? One of the first things you should ask is how long he has had the tractor and where he got it. Also ask, at this point, whether he still has the bill of sale. If he doesn't and has not had the tractor long, he should be willing to go back to the previous owner to get one. If he claims to be the original owner of a fifty-year-old tractor, but doesn't have any of the purchasing paperwork, you'll have to use your best judgment.

Be sure when you get your bill of sale that it includes the correct serial number, or other identification. If the dollar amount is large, or if you are uneasy about the legality of the sale, you might

*The author's work tractor, a 1946 Ford-Ferguson 2N, doing its duty hauling maple sap. Granddaughter Jessica, age four, helps with the gathering.*

consider requiring that your bill of sale be notarized. At least then you will have some recourse if, after you've completed the restoration, you learn you have to give the tractor back.

## Insurance

Once money has changed hands, and you've got the bill of sale, you are the owner. Ordinarily, your homeowner's insurance will be sufficient protection for liabilities during restoration. If you are restoring tractors as a business, however, check with your agent. If you transport the tractor home yourself, your regular truck/trailer insurance should apply to cargo. If the value of your purchase is great, you might be wise to talk to your agent about special coverage for it while in transit, during the restoration process and whenever the completed job performs in parades or other public events. (I once used my antique tractor to pull a church float in a parade. On the float and along the parade route were children, doing unpredictable things, and by the time the parade was over, there had been more-than-fleeting thoughts on the subject of liability.)

---

### Tip: Clean Your Tractor on the Way Home

On the way home with your tractor, you may want to do several things: You may want to have the whole tractor serviced by a place that degreases engines.

This is the ideal time to stop off at a self-service car wash and give the tractor an initial cleaning and degreasing to remove the years of "vintage" mud and oil. Car washes have the high-pressure water wands and drainage that is perfect for this job—you don't want all that grease in your driveway or on your shop floor.

Assuming you have already done your best to operate the tractor to determine its condition, you may want to stop at a service station and have the oil, fuel, anti-freeze and tire liquid drained; you can do this in your own shop and then take the liquid waste to a disposal facility, but for most of us, this can be a messy procedure.

---

# Chapter 3

# Getting Started: Workplace, Tools and Disassembly

**Workplace and Tools**

Tractor restorers come in all sizes and shapes, and so do their workplaces. Some beautifully restored tractors come from unbelievably crowded and cluttered shops, but, as a general rule, the old axiom, "Handsome is, as handsome does," applies. Organizing your shop will eliminate one of the greatest sources of frustration: misplacing parts and tools.

Of course, the more space, the better, but you can get by very well using half of a two-car garage. Hang a sheet of clear plastic down the middle to keep grit, dirt and flying debris off of your car.

For best results, have your workplace set up before you bring in the tractor. You'll need a good workbench with a heavy-duty vise, some storage shelves and pegboard with tool holders. Unless your shop has a ceiling, putting some planks on the ceiling joists will give you excellent storage space for such

things as the hood, grille and fenders. Make sure you have several large trash cans for regularly disposing of such things as oily rags, scrap parts and the boxes new parts come in.

Even if your workplace has plenty of natural light, you should install several large fluorescent light fixtures to help when you're working at night or on cloudy days. You will also need at least two electrical outlets for connecting lights and power tools with extension cords.

A source of heat will be required in most climates, but make sure the type you select is safe. Remember, carbon monoxide will concentrate on the floor, where you will be working a good percentage of the time. The traditional Modine shop heater is hard to beat.

You've always wanted a roll-around tool cabinet and now is your chance to justify it. And don't scrimp

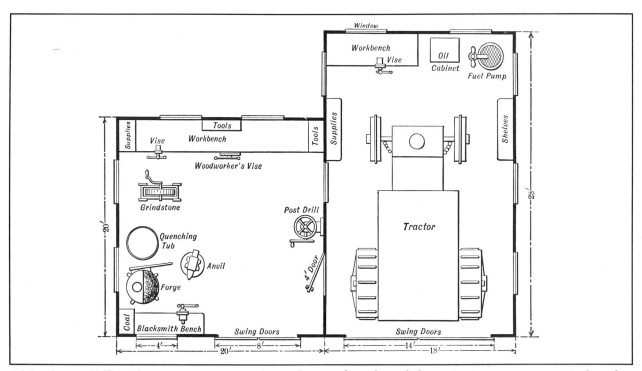

*Advice from a 1913 guide to gas tractor operation and maintenance, here showing the ideal tractor workshop and* *the tools needed to maintain your own tractor in those days of the new technology.*

on tools. A good set of Snap-On or other name-brand wrenches, sockets, ratchets and screwdrivers will well reward you, despite their extra cost. An air compressor and air-powered impact wrench are vital necessities. To do a quality job, you'll also need a torque wrench. For electrical work, you'll need a volt-ohmmeter and point dwell meter/tachometer. Compression and vacuum gauges will complete your required instruments.

You may need some specialized tools for your particular brand of tractor. If a dealership for the brand still exists, you may be able to rent or borrow such tools. If not, contact other collectors or the collectors club. The *I&T Shop Service Manual* for your tractor will often provide a detailed description of a special tool and you can have one made.

## Parts and Data Sources

For a listing of parts houses, reference materials and collectors club newsletters, see the Sources appendix. Most newsletters contain a want ad section you can use to advertise worldwide for hard-to-find

*Mechanic Roger Wywialowski begins engine disassembly on the Farmall A. Having a good shop setup will help you throughout the restoration process.*

*Note the neat, spacious and well-lighted shop area at Machinery Hill. Also note the ample tool chests in the background. Joe Schloskey maintains that good tools are essential to do a quality job; he generally uses Snap-On tools.*

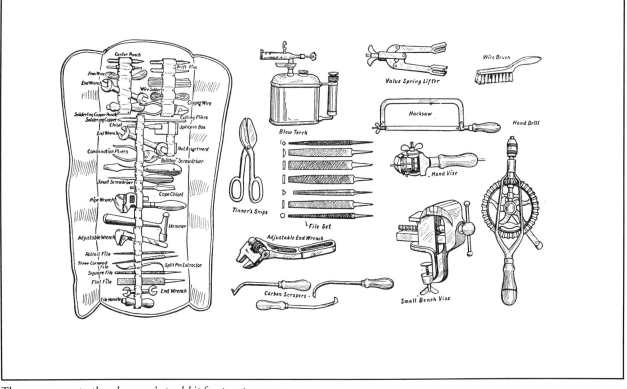

*The consummate thresherman's tool kit for tractor operation and maintenance, circa 1920s.*

parts. The newsletters will also keep you informed of dealer auctions and sales by collectors. Also watch for farm auctions in your area. It will often be worth your while to attend just to pick up the odd part, if not a whole tractor for parts. Become familiar with the "rusty iron shopping centers" (junkyards) in your area, especially those with tractors.

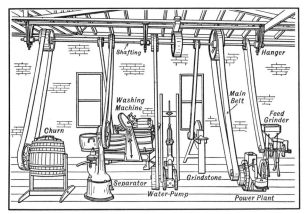

*More advice from the 1913 guide to gas tractor operation and maintenance showing how to set up your own workshop run off of overhead ceiling shafts driving machine tools via belting.*

When all else fails, you can have some fairly elaborate parts made from scratch. Your best bet is to contact other tractor and auto restorers in your area. They can put you in touch with machine shops with phenomenal capabilities. Making a new part will be expensive and time-consuming, but often it is your only recourse. Having the worn out or broken part for a pattern will help considerably.

An auto restorer acquaintance recounts this tale: He delivered the trunk hinges for his rare Jaguar sports car to a plating company for rechroming. When the hinges were returned, however, the pins were missing. The plating people couldn't find them and finally drained the plating tank. There, in the bottom, were the two pins, now ruined. Although the restorer couldn't use the remnants for a pattern, he did have a pretty good idea of what was required, based on the rest of the hinges. Later, at an antique auto swap meet, he found a pair of hinges for an early Mercury automobile, the pins of which were identical to those he needed for the Jaguar. So keep your eyes open for parts sharing.

### Disassembly and Degreasing

Now, assuming you've got your shop set up and your tools organized and your tractor is there, you are ready to go to work. Again, organization will save you time, money and headaches, so plan your work and then work your plan!

If you used the checklist when you bought the tractor, you have a good idea of what the tractor needs. It's best to lay out the repair tasks on a spreadsheet, estimating the time needed for each task. Look for a natural sequence of events so that you don't take off parts you've just installed in order to do another job. A job spreadsheet or flow chart will also identify which parts you should order early so that you'll have them when needed and which parts require scrounging and may take some time to find.

The first work you do on your tractor will likely be removing the sheet metal: hood, fenders, side panels, gas tank and so on. Also remove the grille and radiator, operator's seat, steering wheel, lights, battery and generator. If the wiring is in the form of a harness, it is a good idea to remove it at this point, too.

Now, you can clearly see the extent of grease and grime on your tractor. All evidence of dirt, grease, and field grime must come off before you can do a quality paint job. You will find the worst of these accumulations on steering knuckles, tie rods, the bellhousing, and other hard-to-reach places and behind the carburetor. Soaking these areas with kerosene, WD-40, Gunk or another brand of degreaser for a while will soften the accumulations so that you can remove them with a wire brush and putty knife.

You might consider renting a steam jenny from an equipment rental agency. These machines spray steam and solvents with great effectiveness. Because the steam results in a lot of water residue, several thicknesses of newspaper spread on the floor under the tractor will absorb the grease and moisture.

Some grime can be removed only with sandblasting. Many restorers take the whole tractor to a sandblaster after they have removed the sheet metal. Or, you can buy your own sandblaster fairly inexpensively. In either case, be sure that openings are covered to prevent the sand from getting inside the engine, transmission and so on.

Once you are done blasting and steaming, it will be safe to remove the distributor, carburetor and starter. It's still a good idea to stuff a rag in the manifold and other mounting holes to keep small parts from dropping in. You can degrease small parts separately in a tank of kerosene or solvent such as Stodard Solvent. Lye or caustic soda solutions are also effective, but they are dangerous and hard to dispose of.

Finally, use your air compressor and nozzle to blast out any remaining dirt and to make sure oil and fuel passages are clear.

The last preliminary job will be to take off the wheels to provide easier access to the work. In many cases, however, you may recognize that the tractor will have to be moved in the course of the work, in which case, it may be easier to work around the wheels. Also, if the tractor is going to be split, it may be better to leave the wheels on at least one-half, so that you can roll it away from the other half.

# Chapter 4

# Engine Rebuilding and Restoration

It is the job of the engine to convert the energy of the fuel into useful work. How this gets done, and how to fix it when it isn't getting done, is the subject of this chapter.

In tractors of the types likely to be encountered by the restorer, there can be one-, two-, three-, four-, six-, or even eight-cylinder engines, all of which can run on kerosene, gasoline, LPG (Liquefied Petroleum Gas, or propane) or diesel fuel. Many can run on two of these fuels. Details of the design of these engines may vary widely, but the basic task is the same: to convert the energy of the fuel into useful work.

Most tractors built between 1920 and the 1960s have four-cylinder engines. There are exceptions to this rule, of course: the very successful John Deere line of two-cylinder machines, some early single-cylinder machines, some eight-cylinder diesels and conversions such as the Funk-8N Ford, a few six-cylinder machines such as the Oliver and the crop of three-cylinder diesel and gasoline tractors from the 1960s.

*This very early John Deere D is known as a Spoker because of its spoked flywheel. Such features add materially to collectibility.*

A four-cycle engine (except a radial type, such as used in aircraft) can have any number of cylinders—but as the number increases, so do the complexities. Four cylinders were generally chosen as the best compromise between smoothness and cost.

## Engine Theory

The conversion of fuel energy into useful work follows a sequence of operations known as the engine cycle in each of the cylinders; the more cylinders, the more times the cycle is repeated during each two revolutions of the crankshaft.

The cycle begins with the intake stroke. Either atmospheric pressure or a supercharger fills the cylinder through the open intake valve as the piston moves from the top to the bottom. In the case of a diesel engine, the cylinder is filled with air only. With carburetor engines, it is a mixture of vaporized fuel and air.

As the piston moves up again in the compression stroke, with both the intake and exhaust valves closed, the gas is compressed to a small fraction of its original volume. When the piston is near the top of its stroke, ignition occurs—by means of a spark plug

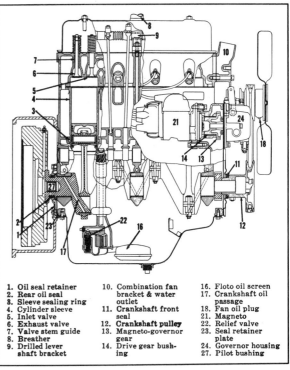

| | | |
|---|---|---|
| 1. Oil seal retainer | 10. Combination fan bracket & water outlet | 16. Floto oil screen |
| 2. Rear oil seal | | 17. Crankshaft oil passage |
| 3. Sleeve sealing ring | 11. Crankshaft front seal | 18. Fan oil plug |
| 4. Cylinder sleeve | | 21. Magneto |
| 5. Inlet valve | 12. Crankshaft pulley | 22. Relief valve |
| 6. Exhaust valve | 13. Magneto-governor gear | 23. Seal retainer plate |
| 7. Valve stem guide | 14. Drive gear bushing | 24. Governor housing |
| 8. Breather | | 27. Pilot bushing |
| 9. Drilled lever shaft bracket | | |

*Sectional view of the Farmall A, B and C Series engine, showing the overhead-valve design. Intertec*

*The John Deere M and L Series were unique in the Deere family of two-cylinder tractors in that they had in-line,* rather than transverse, engines, and foot-operated clutches. Shown here is a Model MT.

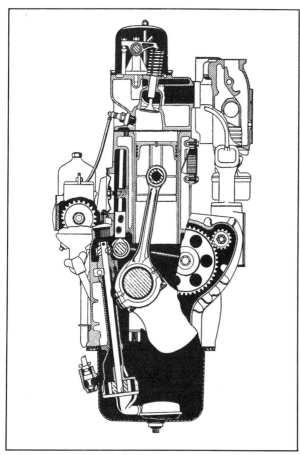

*Frontal view of the Farmall A, B and C Series engine.*
Intertec

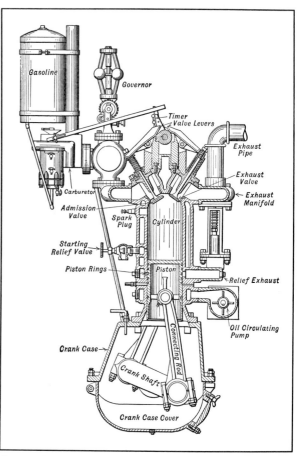

*Sectional view of the Hart-Parr valve-in-head motor with integral cylinder and head.*

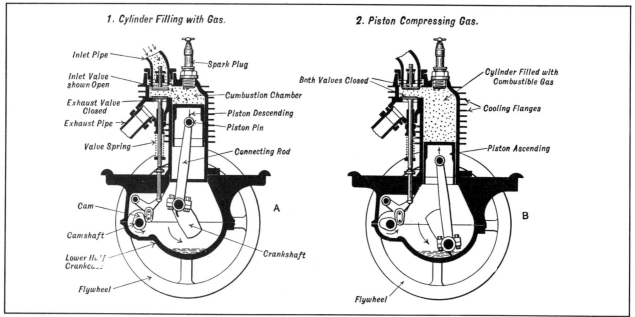

*Sectional view of a simple four-stroke engine showing the method for charging the cylinder with fuel and compressing it prior to ignition.*

with carbureted engines or by means of a squirt of fuel in a diesel. Combustion of the fuel liberates a large amount of heat, most of which is imparted to the gasses of combustion, increasing their pressure.

The power stroke follows, as the expanding gasses force the piston downward. The higher the compression of the intake stroke, the more the molecules are crowded together (which aids in complete combustion); also, more expansion can take place on the power stroke before the pressure falls to the point that no more useful work is being done.

Now, the exhaust valve opens and the piston moves up on the exhaust stroke, forcing out the expanded gasses—and the four-cycle strokes begin again.

This type of engine is known as a four-stroke, or four-cycle engine; you probably will not run into the other type, the two-cycle engine, in tractors except for some which used the GM Detroit Diesel as an alternative to their own engines. The two-cycle engine is common in chain saws and outboard motors for boats, snowmobiles and motorcycles.

## Producing Power

Basically, the power produced by an engine is determined by the number and size of the fuel charges expanded during a unit of time. This basic statement must be tempered by the compression ratio consideration. As the piston moves up and down in the cylinder, receiving, compressing, expanding and exhausting fuel charges, the volume above the piston at the top of the stroke represents a waste: On the intake stroke, such volume is not swept, resulting in a smaller charge; on the compression stroke, the molecules are not as compacted as they could be; on the power stroke, useful pressures disappear sooner; and on the exhaust stroke, not all of the expanded gasses (which are now inert) are expelled. Compression ratios are determined by limitations of the structure and the fuel used, but generally, the higher the compression, the better the use of each fuel charge.

All things being equal, you should get twice the horsepower if you double an engine's speed. For instance, a 200 ci engine running at 4000 rpm should produce the same horsepower as a 400 ci engine at 2000 rpm. The fact that this is not always true is because of three efficiency factors.

The first is "volumetric." Any difference in the theoretical swept volume of the cylinder and the actual size of the charge is the result of air flow losses on the way in. This is best measured by the pressure difference at the time the intake valve closes, from that of either atmospheric or supercharger output pressure. The faster the charge has to move to get in or the number and types of obstacles it encounters on the way contribute to this loss of efficiency.

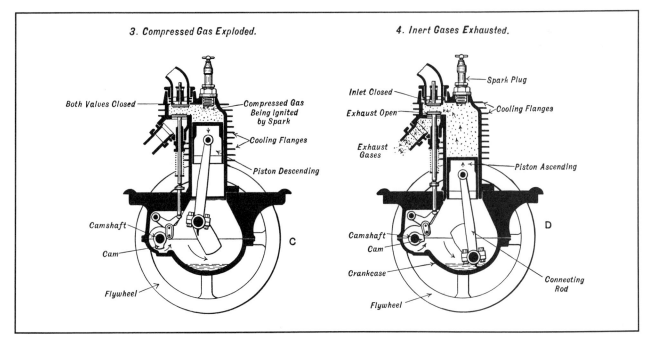

Sectional view of a simple four-stroke engine showing the effect of the ignition explosion and how burnt gases are exhausted from the cylinder.

Next is "thermal" efficiency. This is the difference in the theoretical heat value of the fuel and the amount of heat actually doing the work. Inefficiencies here are the result of incomplete combustion, loss of heat to the cylinder walls and so on.

Last is "mechanical" efficiency. These losses are friction and the portion of developed horsepower used to run the engine itself, such as that required for the valve train, water pump, distributor, fuel-injection pump and oil pump.

What exactly is horsepower? Basically, it is a rate of doing work. Remember, the job of the engine is to convert the fuel energy into useful work; horsepower is the standard of measurement of that work. In technical terms, one horsepower is the amount of work done in lifting 550 pounds one foot in one second.

Most tractor models you are likely to find have been tested at the Nebraska Tractor Testing Laboratory. The horsepower ratings given for a particular model are based on actual observations and do not include correction factors for atmospheric conditions; therefore, Nebraska test data may differ from manufacturer ratings.

Over the years, several terms relating to horsepower have come into common use. Definitions of the various terms were given by H. J. Slothower, a product engineer with International Harvester Company in a 1965 American Society of Agricultural Engineers (ASAE) technical paper. His definitions and explanations are:

### Indicated Horsepower

This is the power developed in the cylinders of the engine. This will be high, and these results are not often quoted in advertisements.

### Gross Horsepower

This is the power measured at the flywheel of a bare or stripped engine not installed in the tractor. In this case, the engine is equipped with only the parts needed to make the engine run.

### Net Horsepower

This is the power obtained at the flywheel while the engine is equipped with all the accessories needed to make it operate by itself.

### PTO Horsepower

This is the measured power obtained at the tractor power takeoff, or PTO. The PTO or belt tests

*An in-tractor engine overhaul underway on the Farmall A. The valve-in-head design of the Farmall's engine lends* *itself to this approach. The engine is almost as accessible as if it were on an engine stand.*

made during the Nebraska Tractor Tests are observed results and do not reflect any corrections.

## Drawbar Horsepower

This is the power available at the drawbar of the tractor to pull equipment. The Nebraska Tractor Tests drawbar ratings are only observed results; no corrections are made for temperature, humidity, barometric pressure or wheel slippage.

## Peak Brake Horsepower

This is the highest horsepower developed without any speed limitation. These runs are often made during a very short time.

## Maximum Intermittent Brake Horsepower

This is considered the maximum saleable horsepower and is usually used when referring to power units.

## Continuous-Brake Horsepower

These ratings are those recommended for operation under continuous conditions. This is used mainly for power unit terminology.

## SAE Horsepower

This formula is intended to determine the approximate brake horsepower of an engine. The formula is bore squared times the number of cylinders, divided by 2.5. SAE (Society of Automotive Engineers) horsepower assumes, among other things, that piston speed is 1,000 feet per minute. This means that short-stroke, high-speed engines are not realistically rated by this method.

For many older tractors, the drawbar horsepower rating was half of the PTO horsepower. Several factors contributed to this. First, the power it took to move these heavy tractors was not available at the drawbar. Second, worm drives such as are used on the Fordson tractor are only around fifty percent efficient. This means that of the power going into a worm drive, half comes out as heat and the other half is usable. Even well-designed and well-built spur and helical gears lose approximately one-half a percent per mesh—so the more gears between the engine and the wheels, the less available power at the drawbar.

Third, gear limitations in early tractor designs made it necessary to limit the drawbar output to less than the tractor could produce. These early tractors

*For a complete show-quality restoration, you will probably want to completely remove the engine from the chassis. Here, the Ford-Ferguson 9N is nearly ready for engine removal. The steering wheel, gas tank, seat, battery and radiator have been removed.*

often had exposed drive gears driving directly onto the wheels. These gears were made as durable as metallurgy of that era could produce, but loads had to be limited to ensure reasonable life.

## Evaluating Your Engine

Hopefully, when you inspected your tractor before buying it, you were able to run the engine. If not, you should include a complete overhaul in your cost estimations. The chances are good that you will want to do this as part of the restoration anyway, so that you are sure of its condition and that you have done a first-class restoration job. If you subscribe to the "If it ain't broke, don't fix it" school of thought, or if the engine has recently been overhauled, you may want to leave it alone.

### Tip: Freeing a Seized Engine

As so often was the case, the tractor you are interested in may have experienced engine failure in the midst of its last harvest season. In such circumstances, a lot of time could not be wasted in troubleshooting or in major repair, so it was time for a new tractor instead. The owner may have had good intentions of fixing it during the winter, but after several winters passed, it was more or less forgotten.

Chances are, the owner doesn't remember, or never knew, the real cause of death. Chances also are, he'll tend to minimize the extent of the repairs required. In any case, the price to restore is almost certainly higher than for an engine that will run.

By proceeding systematically, you can hopefully assess the magnitude of the repairs, and adjust your offer price accordingly. After a cursory external examination to determine if the engine is basically complete and that there are no connecting rods sticking through the crankcase, and after you've checked and noted the pre-starting items on the checklist, the first determination is: Will the engine turn over, or is it stuck?

The phenomena of the stuck engine is more common in antique tractor engines than almost any other major problem. Besides being nasty to deal with in its own right, it may mask other expensive problems, such as bent connecting rods, or even a bad transmission. A seized engine is the result of the pistons adhering to the cylinder walls because of poor lubrication causing the piston to expand during operation and fuse with the cylinder walls; often rust then sets in over time to compound the problem. This is especially likely if the pistons are aluminum and the cylinder walls are cast iron.

What courses of action are available when a stuck engine is encountered? If your tractor is a common one, the easiest course may be to just buy a replacement engine.

But, before you get to that point, see if you can determine why it's stuck. Use a hand crank; or jack up one rear wheel and with the transmission in high gear, see if the engine is seized hard or if it feels spongy. A spongy feeling indicates something other than seized pistons, unless the rods are already badly distorted. Spongy stuck may be caused by a jammed valve or by liquid—such as oil, fuel, coolant and so on—filling the cylinders above the pistons. To cure the latter, remove the spark plugs and try turning it over.

Next, remove the oil pan drain plug, and with a flashlight try to observe the condition of the cylinder walls. If they are shiny, continue. If you see copious rust, count on a complete disassembly.

Freeing a stuck engine takes either lots of patience or lots of pressure—hydraulic pressure. The ultimate way to free an engine is to take it to a machine shop and have the pistons pressed out. Before getting to that point, though, you should try to soak it free by filling the cylinders, through the spark plug holes, with a penetrating oil straight, or in solution with another agent. Don't put the plugs back in tight; simply insert them loosely.

Some people mix brake fluid with penetrating oil or some automatic transmission fluid. Palmer Fossum prefers a mixture of penetrating oil and kerosene. Others recommend straight olive oil, Hoppe's #9 gun solvent, or even Sloan's Liniment. One of the best I have found is Marvel Mystery Oil. Whatever you choose, the idea is to soak a little lubricant down with the rust to dissolve the bond.

This can take a long time. If you can wait, it can take a year. Periodically, give it a try with the hand crank, or with the jacked-up back wheel, which can go back or forth. If the spark plug holes are over the pistons, it may be possible to insert a brass rod, and tap on the top of the pistons, pounding with a wooden or plastic hammer to encourage the oil to find its way down and to jar things loose.

Finally, remove the head and pan, then disconnect the connecting rods. Use a hardwood rod, such as an ax handle or a baseball bat directly on top of the piston, tapping with a sledgehammer. If this fails, at least you've got a good start at dismantling it for its trip to the machine shop.

Through all this, you are probably thinking about the possibility of breaking it loose by towing the tractor and popping the clutch. Many have been freed this way after a period of soaking, but many engines and clutches have also been ruined this way, so proceed cautiously if you choose this method. First, check with other collectors or the collectors club to see if the engine is generally strong enough to survive the procedure. Next, be absolutely sure it isn't a stuck starter ring gear or something other than seized pistons. Finally, use high gear, go slowly, and do the procedure on dirt that will allow some sliding of the wheels.

If, when you evaluated your tractor, you could run the engine, you could assure yourself that at least the engine was complete and that major parts, such as the crankshaft, were not broken.

## Troubleshooting

If the engine is operable, listen for unevenness in the exhaust; this could indicate that one (or more) of the cylinders is not firing. Listen for knocking sounds, especially when the throttle is quickly closed; this could indicate loose connecting rod bearings. Look for low oil pressure; this could indicate either a worn oil pump or loose main bearings. Look for blue smoke from the exhaust or crankcase breather; this could indicate blow-by in the piston rings.

A compression check will tell you about the condition of the valves and piston rings. For carbureted engines, first remove all the spark plugs and open the throttle. Then, with the compression gauge inserted into one of the plug holes, crank the engine either by hand or with the starter. Get a reading for each cylinder; readings should be within ten percent of each other and within the acceptable pressure range for the particular engine.

To help determine what is causing a low reading, the valves or the rings, pour a small amount of engine oil into the spark plug hole and repeat the test. The oil will make a temporary seal around leaky rings, so if pressure improves, you know that the valves for that cylinder are OK. A blown head gasket may also produce low readings when oil is added. Be wary of this if two adjacent cylinders are low.

Checking the compression of a diesel engine is basically the same procedure, except you remove the injectors instead of the spark plugs. Because the compression is higher, you will need either a special compression gauge or a diesel adapter. Be sure to shut off fuel to the injector pump, and don't forget to remove the washer from the injector hole; you'll need new washers when re-installing the injectors.

It may not be necessary to remove the engine to completely overhaul it. Many tractors have removable piston sleeves, so you won't need to rebore the cylinders on those engines. If the engine is of the overhead-valve or valve in-head design, you can take the head to the machine shop to have the valves done. With the valve-in-block design, you can hand-grind the valve seats, if necessary, but it's better to take the engine block to the machine shop.

*Mechanic Ken Moravec uses a breaker bar to loosen the head bolts of Ford-Ferguson 9N. It's a good idea to loosen head bolts a quarter turn at a time in the same sequence as prescribed for tightening, thus lessening the chance for warping the head.*

---

### Tip: Tracking Down Engine Failures

If the engine won't run, but is not stuck, then it's a simple process of elimination. Check for ignition, compression, vaporized fuel and timing, following the troubleshooting guides in the respective chapters.

Of the preceding, timing is the most difficult to ascertain. Timing that is off the mark can be the result of mixed-up plug wires, stripped timing (camshaft) or distributor drive gears, broken or loose timing chain, incorrect distributor adjustment, or incorrect assembly.

Step one is logically to get your timing light and to see if timing can be set to the specification. If this is accomplished, and it's still not right, check the plug wiring again, and then check for correct meshing of the camshaft gear to the crankshaft. There is generally a mark on the gears to indicate correct assembly; check the *I&T Shop Service Manual* for details.

The cylinder head removed from the 9N. Palmer Fossum found that the engine was so worn that the pistons could be moved around in the cylinders with little effort. Obviously, a complete rebuild was in order.

Moravec was able to slide the engine off of the 9N without the aid of a hoist. He placed it on the blocks to facilitate removal of the clutch.

## Engine Disassembly

Regardless of whether you intend to remove the engine from the tractor, there are some preliminary jobs you must do. If you didn't remove the oil, fuel and coolant when you brought the tractor home, you must now. Next, remove the hood, grille, fuel tank and radiator. Now the engine is exposed, almost like it was on an engine stand. If the engine still has grease and dirt on it, get as much off as possible before going any further. You must remove the valve cover and detach any accessories bolted to the engine, such as the coil or spark plug wire looms.

It's a good idea to tag the spark plug wires before removing them; it is strange how some wires could go either of two places once you take your eyes off them. You should also remove the spark plugs at this time, since the head is still attached; if you wait until later, you will have a difficult time holding on to the head to remove the plugs.

If your engine has its valves in the head, you should remove the intake and exhaust manifolds to remove the head. You can leave them on and just disconnect the exhaust pipe and carburetor attachments, but be aware that the head is already quite heavy and ungainly.

Now, with a carefully fitted socket wrench and a breaker bar, loosen the head bolts following the same pattern prescribed for tightening down the head. Start with a quarter-turn on each for the first pass, then a half-turn on the second. This will relieve the stresses built up in the head and prevent warping or cracking. Don't worry if the stud comes out with the head bolt, but as soon as you can, remove the nut by placing the stud in your vise and taking the torch to the nut; then put the stud back into the block to prevent dirt and grime from getting into the holes.

When all the nuts are off, try lifting the head. Some gentle prying should cause it to come loose, but try to pry against the head gasket, rather than the block (the head gasket will be thrown away, anyway). If this fails, try putting back the two end spark plugs and turning the engine over either by the starter or by hand-cranking. A 6.0:1 compression ratio and a 3.75 in. diameter piston will generate almost 1,000

*After the engine was out of the tractor, the next order of business was to remove the clutch.*

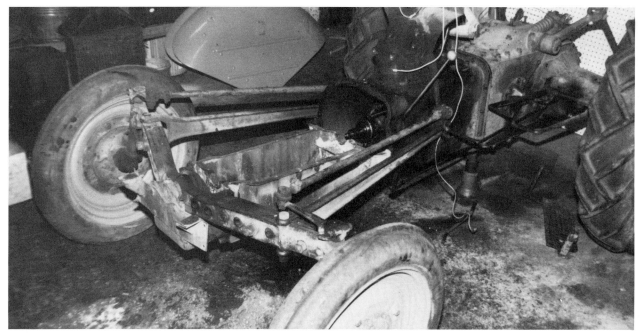

Taking the oil pan off of the engine of the Ford-Ferguson 9N and reinstalling it on the tractor allowed for the reattach-
ment of the front wheels. This facilitated moving the tractor around the shop during the restoration process.

The 9N engine is mounted on an engine stand to begin disassembly. The first step is the removal of the valves.

The easiest way to completely clean the engine block is to have it professionally done in a hot chemical bath. First, the engine was completely disassembled, then the block was sent out. Randy Helbling, shop manager at the Northfield, Minnesota, NAPA auto parts store, prepares to immerse the engine from the Ford-Ferguson 9N into the solvent bath.

pounds of lift. You may also want to put on two or three nuts as well, finger tight, to restrain the head—especially if you use the starter.

Next, remove the oil pan. If the pan is of cast material, it's a good idea to do a patterned loosening of the bolts, as you did for the head, to prevent warpage. Look for any loose parts or chunks of metal in the oil pan. They are clues to what you will be dealing with later.

## Top End Overhaul

Once the head is off, you are ready to do the valve job. You will want to remove as much carbon from the head and tops of the pistons as possible before proceeding. Try to keep carbon from getting into the cylinders and into water or oil passages. Inspect push rods, camshaft, rockers and related parts for wear or damage, and replace them as necessary.

Next, if your engine is a valve-in-block type, crank it over a few turns to see that all the valves are operating properly. If you are not familiar with the

*After the engine block comes out of the solvent bath and is completely rinsed clean, a long, stiff-bristle brush is used to ensure that oil galleries are open and free of contamination. Dirty oil passages are one of the surest ways of building in premature wear and failure.*

*Dipping the engine into the hot solvent for a minimum of twenty-four hours not only strips the exterior of grease,* *grime and paint, it dissolves gasket material, oil sludge, carbon and varnish from exterior and interior surfaces.*

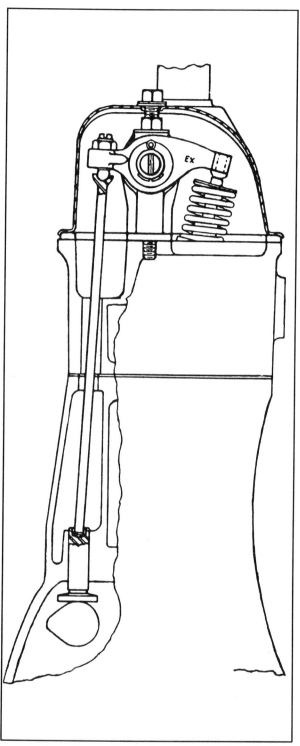

mechanism, make a sketch of the arrangement of springs, clips, washers, guides and adjusting nuts before disassembling anything.

Using a valve spring compressor, remove the clip, or keeper, from the slot at the base of the valve stem. The valve is now free to be removed. Repeat this process with each valve, keeping track of where they came from. If any of the valves have notches or burned sections, you will need to replace them. If your tractor is an orphan, take the old valve to the parts store, to see whether it can be matched from stock.

For valves that are in fairly good condition, you can match-grind them into their own seats by spreading valve compound on the seat, reinserting the valve and then rotating it against the seat with a valve-grinding tool (available from most tool rental shops). You can also take the valves to a machine shop and have them resurfaced.

If the valve seats are removable, you should also replace them unless they are in extremely good condition. It's a good idea to hand-lap them against their own seats, anyway, to ensure a tight seal.

While you are working on the valves, have the springs, clips and so on, soaking in kerosene or solvent, so that they are ready for reinstallation. Look for any evidence of wear on the guides and camshaft and replace as necessary. Then reassemble in the reverse order of removal.

*A typical overhead-valve engine valvetrain, here from an Allis-Chalmers. Adjustments are made by removing the rocker cover and loosening the nut above the push rod. A screwdriver slot is provided to turn the stem for the adjustment. With the engine running, a flat feeler gauge inserted between the valve and the rocker (above the spring) will indicate when the correct clearance has been achieved by turning the screwdriver. Re-tighten the locking nut. Intertec*

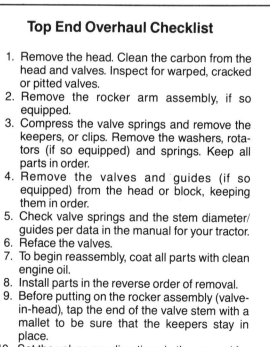

**Top End Overhaul Checklist**

1. Remove the head. Clean the carbon from the head and valves. Inspect for warped, cracked or pitted valves.
2. Remove the rocker arm assembly, if so equipped.
3. Compress the valve springs and remove the keepers, or clips. Remove the washers, rotators (if so equipped) and springs. Keep all parts in order.
4. Remove the valves and guides (if so equipped) from the head or block, keeping them in order.
5. Check valve springs and the stem diameter/guides per data in the manual for your tractor.
6. Reface the valves.
7. To begin reassembly, coat all parts with clean engine oil.
8. Install parts in the reverse order of removal.
9. Before putting on the rocker assembly (valve-in-head), tap the end of the valve stem with a mallet to be sure that the keepers stay in place.
10. Set the valves per directions in the manual for your tractor.

The procedure is much the same for valve-in-head engines. You must remove the rocker assemblies before you can get at the valves. Compress the spring with a spring tool and remove the keeper, or clip, holding the valve. Keep springs, clips, guides and such parts separated with the valve they were on. You can then hand-grind the valves into their seats, just as with the valve-in-block type.

Especially with the valve-in-head type, this work is most easily done at a machine shop, and the quality and time saved easily justify the cost.

**Bottom End Overhaul**

Once you are into it this far, you may as well do a complete job on your engine. At least check the bearings and rings to be sure that they are "within

## Cams

A cam is a device where the distance from the cam surface to some reference point or surface serves as a control or actuation signal. Cams are used to trigger on-off responses in machines or to position a device in response to the motion of another device. The most common type of cam is the flat plate cam which, as the name implies, is a contour cut from flat stock. A radial cam uses rotary motion as an input; a translating cam uses straight-line motion as an input. The "signal" or position of the cam surface is read off the cam by a device called a cam follower.

Cam followers can be constrained to respond with straight-line motion aligned through the cam center of rotation (radial follower), straight-line motion aligned off the center of rotation (offset follower), or by rotation about a swinging follower arm (swinging follower). The swinging follower minimizes the pressure between cam and follower and thus is often preferred with small cam radii.

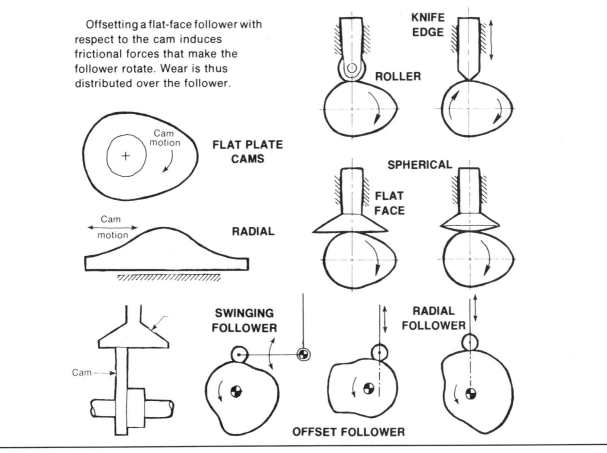

Offsetting a flat-face follower with respect to the cam induces frictional forces that make the follower rotate. Wear is thus distributed over the follower.

*Types of cams.*

During any complete engine rebuild, it makes sense to magnaflux your engine casings to check for cracks in the metal that are not visible to the naked eye. This is the magnaflux machine at work at NAPA. Checking the block and head for cracks prior to rebuilding will save the time and money that could be spent rebuilding a faulty block.

It takes neither zyglow nor magnaflux to observe the crack in this cylinder. This engine is suitable only for the junkyard.

The old-fashioned mushroom-stemmed valves of the type used in Ford-Ferguson 9N serial number 357. It was not possible to chuck this type of valve in Northfield NAPA's valve grinding machine, so later-model valves were used in rebuilding serial number 357. These incorporated valve rotators, not found on the original, but they were enough of an improvement that Palmer Fossum elected to go with them.

spec." If convenient, this is a good time to remove the engine and mount it to an engine stand (available from most auto parts stores). This is not absolutely necessary, but will make things a lot easier. For some tractors, the engine must be removed before the crankshaft can be removed.

If the main bearings supporting the crankshaft are removable without removing the crankshaft (check the *I&T Shop Service Manual*), you may not need to remove the crankshaft, unless the bearing journals are out of round, or badly scored. If this is the case, remove the crankshaft and take it to a machine shop for regrinding. Then get thicker bearings to make up the difference.

Remember, every time you remove something that moves with the crankshaft, you should replace it in the same position, for both balance and timing purposes. Also, any of the high-tensile bolts, such as those holding the main bearings in place, should be

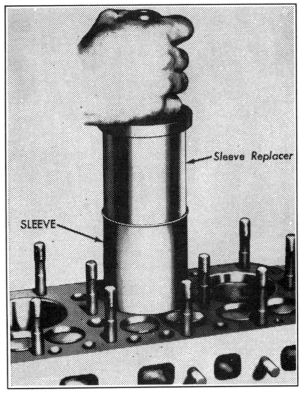

*The use of a piloted mandrel is helpful when replacing sleeves, to prevent sleeve buckling.*

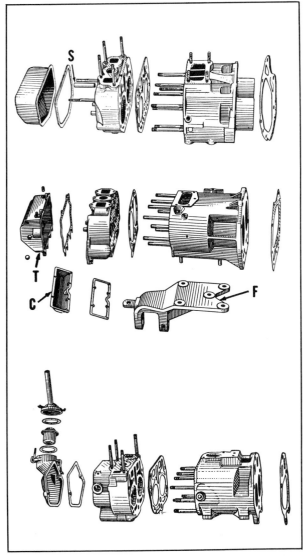

*Exploded view of a two-cylinder John Deere Model D cylinder block. The rocker arm shaft is retained in the tappet case (T). The front end support (F) is bolted to the bottom face of the cylinder.* Intertec

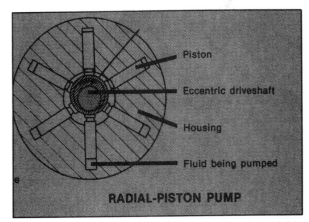

*There are several types of radial piston pumps available, with either regular pistons or ball pistons. Generally, the piston block rotates around a stationary cam, or eccentric, allowing for the use of standard kidney-shaped inlet and exhaust ports. On those where the block is stationary and the shaft rotates, check valves and manifolds are required.*

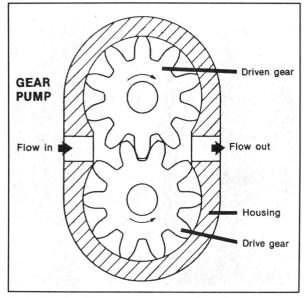

Basic side-by-side gear pump, consisting of two spur gears rotating inside a housing. Fluid is carried by the gear teeth from the inlet to the outlet.

loosened a quarter-turn each, to relieve the stress and avoid warping the bearing cap.

Main and connecting rod bearings are similar and should be removed for inspection in the same way. Look for signs of burning, scoring and wear. You can determine wear by looking at the bearing half edgewise; if it is thinner in the center (most wear is at the bottom center) or if the oil groove is worn away, it needs to be replaced.

Once you have removed the connecting rod bearings, you can push the pistons up and out the top of the block. You may need to remove the ridge from the top of the cylinder first, with a ridge cutter. If, as the pistons clear the cylinder, the rings protrude from their grooves, they were probably doing their job. This is not the time to save a little money, however, so buy a new set of rings.

Check the pistons for conformance to the manufacturer's specifications. Be aware that some makes offered high-compression pistons for use at higher

The valve grinding machine at the Northfield NAPA. Properly refaced, the valves will give life and performance equivalent to new valves.

*Valve grinding requires rotation of the valve against the rotating grinding wheel while maintaining the precise seat angle.*

*For good valve sealing during the combustion process, you will want to lap the valve seats. The first step is to resurface the seats in the valve-in-block engine of the Ford-Ferguson.*

altitudes (usually, above 5,000 feet above sea level). If you are interested in antique tractor pulls or dynamometer demonstrations, you might get these to get a little more than stock horsepower. You might also look into oversized sleeves and pistons.

Now check the cylinder for wear and condition. Since most tractors have replaceable sleeves, or liners, reboring will not be necessary. Removal will be somewhat different for each brand of tractor, so check the manual for directions.

A good major overhaul requires inspection of the oil pump and cleaning of the oil passages. For some tractors, you will have to remove the flywheel to get the pump out. You are likely to find one of two types of oil pumps: the vane type and the gear type.

For the vane oil pump, inspect the condition of the vanes and the surface they operate against. There will be a vane spring compression force specified in the *I&T Shop Service Manual*.

*With the seats resurfaced, the valves are hand-lapped to form a good sealing combination. Valve grinding compound is applied to the interface, then the valve is inserted, but not attached. The suction cup device is then stuck to the valve and rotated back and forth between the palms of the hands. This provides microscopic mating of the two surfaces to ensure leakfree operation.*

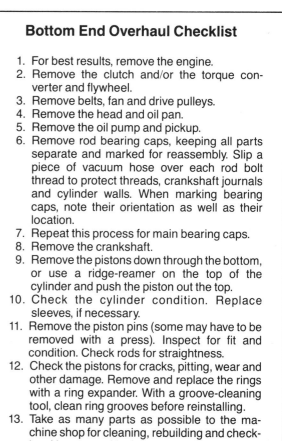

## Bottom End Overhaul Checklist

1. For best results, remove the engine.
2. Remove the clutch and/or the torque converter and flywheel.
3. Remove belts, fan and drive pulleys.
4. Remove the head and oil pan.
5. Remove the oil pump and pickup.
6. Remove rod bearing caps, keeping all parts separate and marked for reassembly. Slip a piece of vacuum hose over each rod bolt thread to protect threads, crankshaft journals and cylinder walls. When marking bearing caps, note their orientation as well as their location.
7. Repeat this process for main bearing caps.
8. Remove the crankshaft.
9. Remove the pistons down through the bottom, or use a ridge-reamer on the top of the cylinder and push the piston out the top.
10. Check the cylinder condition. Replace sleeves, if necessary.
11. Remove the piston pins (some may have to be removed with a press). Inspect for fit and condition. Check rods for straightness.
12. Check the pistons for cracks, pitting, wear and other damage. Remove and replace the rings with a ring expander. With a groove-cleaning tool, clean ring grooves before reinstalling.
13. Take as many parts as possible to the machine shop for cleaning, rebuilding and checking. Have any critical parts Magnafluxed, or its equivalent, before reassembling. Make sure that the new sleeves have the glaze broken with a hone, and that the new rings are installed with their gaps staggered.
14. Coat all sliding and bearing surfaces with clean motor oil before reassembling. Also replace crankshaft oil seals before beginning reassembly.
15. Reassemble in the reverse order, taking note of the marks on pistons, connecting rods and bearing caps, indicating assembly orientation (see manual). Use a piston ring compressing tool, so that the rings slide easily into the cylinder. Use the vacuum hose on the rod studs again to prevent damage.
16. When reassembled, check bearing clearances with Plastigage, or equivalent, going by the directions on the package.
17. Use a torque wrench, and the specified torque, wherever applicable.

*A lapped Ford 9N valve, ready for final installation. Note the swirl pattern honed into the newly installed piston sleeves.*

*The valves and springs are assembled into the head and then the valve clearance is set. Note that the job here requires a special set of Ford tools.*

*A thin open-end wrench is needed to loosen and tighten valve retention nuts.*

There are two types of gear pumps: two gears, side-by-side, called a gear pump; and two gears, one inside the other, called a gerotor pump. They function in the same manner, entrapping oil in the non-meshing teeth and carrying it from the intake side to the pressure side. Gear backlash and tooth-housing clearance will be specified in the manual. Check the ball-spring relief valve, as well.

## Project Tractors

When the head was removed from the Ford-Ferguson 9N engine, the pistons could be moved around in the cylinders. Thus, it was apparent that a complete overhaul was in order. The pan, crankshaft and pistons were removed while the engine was still attached to the back half of the tractor. The front wheels had already been disconnected and rolled away. The basic block was now light enough that it could be handled by hand.

All parts were then taken to the local Northfield, Minnesota, NAPA Auto Parts, where Randy Helbling did the refurbishment. He removed the valves and

*The valve-in-block engine of serial number 357 with the valves freshly reinstalled.*

seats and put the engine block into a tank for a thorough cleaning. When removed from the cleaning tank, the sleeves were replaced, new pistons and rings were installed and all new bearings were installed. The valves were refaced and mated to new seats. The crankshaft was reground, so thicker bearings were used.

When the engine was disassembled, it was found to have valve rotators and later configuration valves installed; serial number 357 would not have had rotators when built. Palmer Fossum gave some thought to the correctness of this configuration, but in the end, decided to leave the rotators in, since they represent such an improvement.

For the Farmall A, an in-tractor engine overhaul was done. It was not necessary to remove the crankshaft. New pistons, sleeves, rings and bearings were installed. A top end overhaul was done using a high-speed grinder especially made for that purpose.

Before reassembly, the piston sleeves were slightly roughed up with a hone, to break the glaze.

*Marsh begins cutting the new seats in the Farmall's cylinder head. Note how well he has organized his work with the valves inserted into a board in the background to make certain he replaces each valve in the place it came from. This helps ensure proper balance in the engine.*

*Cutting new valve seats in the head of the overhead-valve Farmall A engine follows the same procedure as with the Ford 9N's valve-in-block engine. Machinery Hill mechanic Tom Marsh begins the operation by squirting some cutting lube on the valve seat tool guide before grinding the seats.*

*The Farmall A's engine is rated at 18 hp, which is not a lot when driving a 5 ft. mower. Therefore, extra care is taken with valve seating to ensure lasting power.*

A compression test on the Farmall A indicated that the rings were not worn to the point where replacement was necessary, but Schloskey elected to replace rings and cylinder liners anyway, to ensure a quality job. Liner (or sleeve) seals tend to dry out and subsequently leak when left exposed to the atmosphere, so the liners and seal were replaced just before reassembly.

Mechanic Roger Wywialowski pulls the pistons. A check of the bearings indicated that the crankshaft did not have to be removed.

This allows the new rings to seat properly. Although the old sleeves were still serviceable, new sleeve seals were installed, as these are "wet sleeves" on the Farmall A. Joe Schloskey says anytime an engine like this is opened up for any length of time, the sleeve seals dry out, and it's a good idea to replace them.

On both tractors, the oil pumps were judged to be in good condition, but were overhauled anyway.

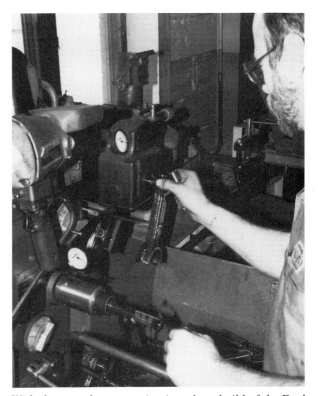

*With the care that was going into the rebuild of the Ford 9N, a complete piston and connecting rod overhaul only made sense. As part of the procedure, shop manager Randy Helbling hones connecting rod bearing inserts at NAPA.*

*Joe Schloskey removes the piston rings from the Farmall A's pistons. Care must be exercised to avoid scratching the sides of the pistons.*

*The cylinder bores of the Ford 9N were then honed to ensure a good seal between the piston rings and the cylinder walls.*

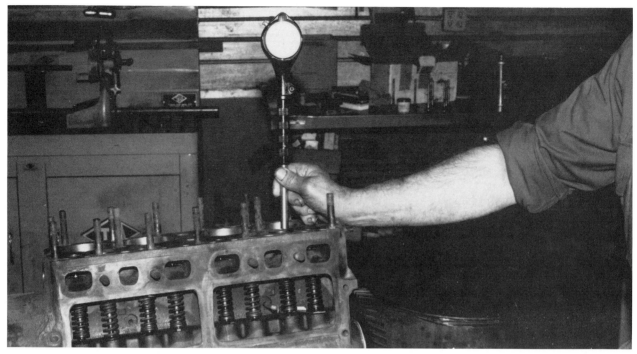

*A dial bore gauge was then used to check for piston clearance.*

*The cylinder head of the Ford-Ferguson 9N was milled to ensure a flat surface that would mate well with the engine block for a good seal. Here is the NAPA plane mill at work.*

*Approximately 0.002 in. were milled off of the head face to ensure flatness.*

*The oil pump for the Ford-Ferguson 9N required new bearing inserts, which in turn required honing to the exact size of the pump shaft.*

*The rebuilt oil gear pump from the engine of Ford-Ferguson 9N. Oil enters the far gallery from the pan, is entrained in the gear teeth and is carried around the outside of the two cutouts to the near gallery and then to the distribution system.*

*Oil filter housings. The one on the right was installed on Ford-Ferguson serial number 357 when Fossum found it. The correct filter, which was installed during the restoration, is shown on the left. This indicates the lengths one must go to in the quest for originality in restoring a show tractor.*

*The Farmall A engine reassembled and ready to go. The engine, as well as the rest of the tractor, will be sandblasted prior to painting.*

*Serial number 357's engine is back in place with the rebuilt governor installed. Note the manifold ports are still cov-* *ered: final engine painting will be done before installation of these parts.*

# Chapter 5

# Carburetor Fuel Systems

Tractor carburetor fuel systems are relatively simple, compared to modern automotive fuel-injection systems, or even automotive carburetor fuel systems. For almost all cases of the type of tractor being considered here, the fuel tank is mounted above the engine, and the fuel is fed to the carburetor by gravity, eliminating the need for a fuel pump. Generally, also, there is only a sediment bowl in the line and no fuel filter. Carburetors, too, are simpler. There is usually no accelerator pump and no automatic choke, and the only external adjustments are the main jet and the idle fuel-air mixture. Internal adjustment is limited to bending the float stem to establish the correct float level. Details for each tractor can be found in the *I&T Shop Service Manual*.

There are three basic types of carburetor fuel system: kerosene, gasoline and Liquefied Petroleum Gas (LPG) or propane. Diesel systems, which are by no means simple, will be addressed separately.

**Fuels and Fuel Systems**

The energy to operate the tractor comes solely from the fuel—be it kerosene, gasoline or LPG—which is metered into the incoming air by the

*The Hercules engine of this 1939 Cletrac General GG featured a common Tillotson carburetor. This engine could produce around 20 hp.*

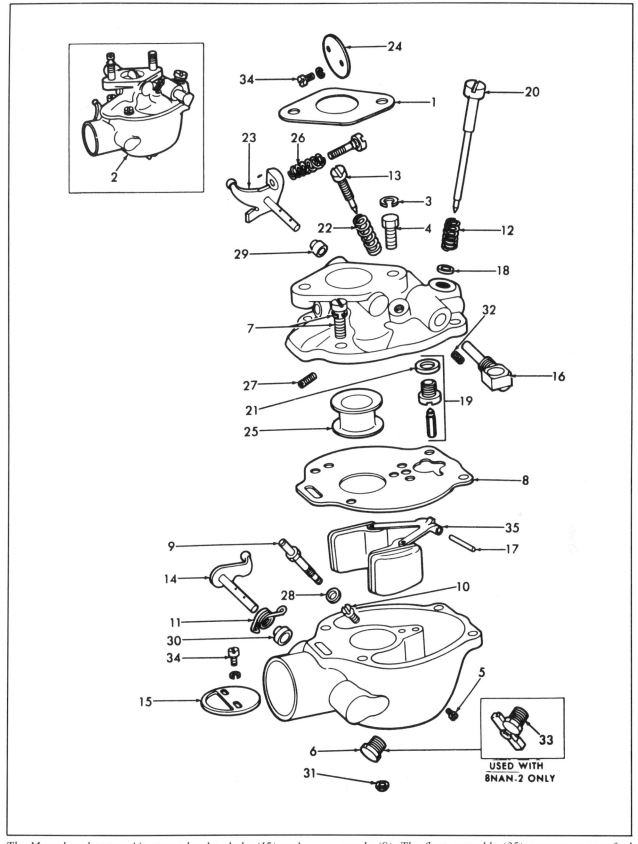

*The Marvel carburetor. Air enters by the choke (15) and exits by the throttle plate (24). Fuel is injected by the main nozzle (9). The float assembly (35) assures correct fuel level.*

USED WITH
8NAN-2 ONLY

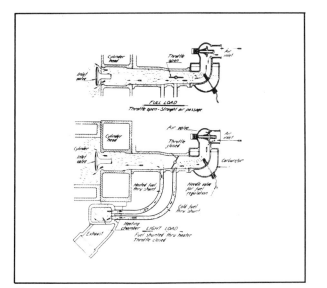

*Shunt carburetor as used on Hart-Parr tractors.*

carburetor. Approximately twenty-one percent of the air is oxygen, which supports the combustion in the cylinders of the engine. The rest of the air consists of inert gasses, mostly nitrogen, which helps prevent combustion temperatures from exceeding practical limits.

The molecules that make up the three kinds of fuels have several different chemical and physical properties, although all are hydrocarbons. The more carbon atoms in the compound, the more energy, or heat value. Fuel that evaporates (changes from a liquid to a gas) easily at room temperature is said to be volatile. Volatile fuel, such as gasoline, is composed of very small hydrocarbon molecules. LPG is even more volatile, because it is already evaporated at room temperature. LPG, in fact, begins to boil at minus 44 degrees Fahrenheit, given normal atmospheric pressure. Kerosene is composed of larger hydrocarbon molecules and is therefore less volatile. The evaporation rate of any fuel increases as the temperature increases or as pressure decreases.

### Gasoline Systems

Liquid fuel must be completely evaporated and mixed with the incoming air to function properly in the engine. For gasoline-fueled engines, some of this vaporization occurs in the venturi throat of the carburetor. The venturi acts to increase the speed of the incoming air as it passes through the restricted area, thereby reducing its pressure. Fuel from the carburetor float chamber is drawn into the stream by the low pressure and is atomized (converted into a fine spray) immediately. It is further vaporized in the intake manifold by exhaust heat (the intake and ex-

haust manifolds are nested together) if the engine has been running.

Final vaporization occurs on the compression stroke due to the heat of compression. A compression ratio of 6.0:1 raises the temperature of the mixture in the cylinder head area by around 350 degrees Fahrenheit.

Thus, by the time ignition occurs, the fuel-air mixture should be completely gaseous. Proper carburetion has resulted in a mixture ratio of about 15:1 by weight.

### LPG Systems

For LPG engines, evaporation must take place in the fuel tank. Remember, LPG boils at minus 44 degrees Fahrenheit, so under normal conditions, as soon as the tank is filled, boiling occurs until the pressure in the tank builds to the point where it stops. Thus, pressure in the tank will vary with outside temperature. At minus 20 degrees Fahrenheit, boiling stops at about 13 psi. At 100 degrees, tank pressure will increase to around 190 psi. From this, it can be seen that LPG equipment may not be the best choice for an Antarctic expedition.

Nevertheless, for most situations, LPG is fine. The function of the LPG carburetor is simply the mixing of the two gasses (fuel and air) in the proper proportion. Now, instead of encouraging manifold heating, the opposite is desired.

### Kerosene Systems

Being the least volatile, kerosene presents the greatest evaporation problem. While the kerosene carburetor functions in the same manner as that for gasoline, more of the vaporization occurs in the hot manifold. For reasons to be discussed later, compression ratios for kerosene engines have to be lower than for equivalent gasoline engines, which puts a further burden on the manifold to do the vaporization.

If a hot manifold is necessary, how do you get the engine started? Therein lies a problem. Most of the kerosene tractors you are likely to see are started on gasoline, and then when everything is hot, a switchover is made. On some early tractors, the manifold had to be heated with a blow torch. Some kerosene carburetors are vaporizer models, wherein exhaust gas is actually directed into heat exchangers that heat the incoming fuel-air charge directly. Some have levers on the manifold that can be set for more exhaust flow during cold weather.

So, why use kerosene at all? It all goes back to the days before engines. People demanded a better lamp than oil lamps and candles. A Canadian chemist, Abraham Gesner, patented a distilling process to produce a fuel for the wick-and-chimney lamp: It was called kerosene. Gesner also refined the liquid from coal, and so it is sometimes referred to as "coal oil." Kerosene is also called "distillate" or "paraffin." It is also known as Jet A, the present commercial jet fuel, and as JP-5 by the military.

Nevertheless, at first, kerosene was all that was available. Later, when catalytic cracking processes were invented to produce gasoline, gas was considered too expensive for tractor use at around fifteen cents per gallon, so kerosene was still the economical fuel of choice.

Another reason for using kerosene is that it has more Btu per gallon than gasoline or LPG. But this, in turn, causes another problem: too much heat.

The mixture of about fifteen parts of air required for each part of gasoline makes a mixture richer than stoichiometric. A stoichiometric mixture is ideal for complete combustion. In an engine, however, such a mixture throughout the combustion chamber would produce temperatures that would be much too high. Therefore, some of the fuel that is taken in, along with the inert components in the air, serve to keep combustion temperatures down. This accounts for

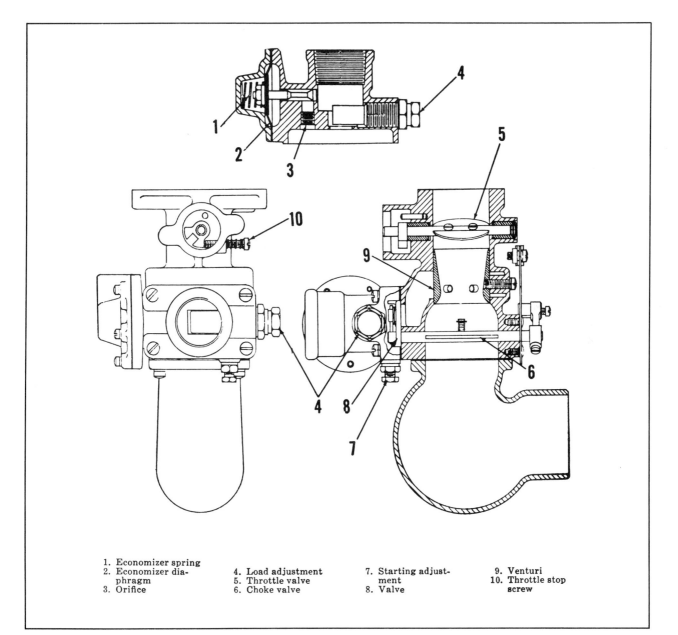

1. Economizer spring
2. Economizer diaphragm
3. Orifice
4. Load adjustment
5. Throttle valve
6. Choke valve
7. Starting adjustment
8. Valve
9. Venturi
10. Throttle stop screw

*Ensign carburetor as used on Farmall LPG tractors.*
Intertec

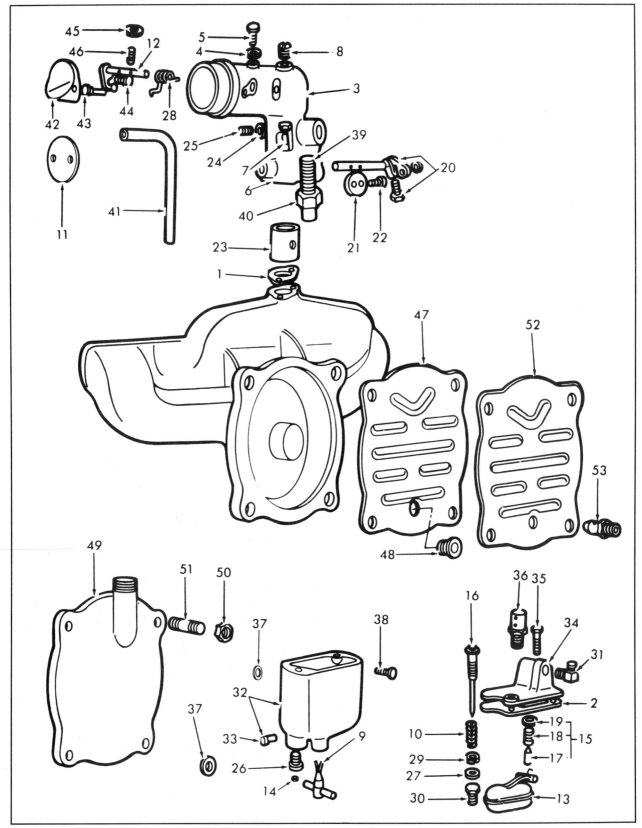

*Kerosene vaporizer carburetor of the type used on the NAN Series Fords. Air and fuel are mixed in the carburetor (3) and then are carried to the drum-like device integral with* *the exhaust manifold, where they are converted into a vapor by the heat and then conducted to the intake manifold.*

the pollution problems associated with engines that run on the rich side of stoichiometric. Diesels, on the other hand, run on the lean side—but we will get into that later.

This, then, was the big problem with kerosene engines. If you wanted them to have a reasonable compression ratio, you had to run them extremely rich to limit combustion temperatures. Lower compression ratios, in the order of 4.0:1, worked well enough, but since heat of compression was low, they were hard to start—although easier to hand-crank. Even at that ratio, fuel consumption could be as much as twenty-five percent higher to do the same amount of work. Some kerosene tractors used water-injection schemes to cool combustion temperatures while the engine was under heavy load.

Some brands of tractors did better on kerosene than others. John Deere, for example, used it with great success on its famous two-cylinder models. During World War II, some other tractor brands were converted to operate on kerosene to alleviate gasoline shortages. These conversions left a lot to be desired, and most were later converted back to gas.

## Carburetor Terminology and Functions

Carburetors for liquid fuels function by using differential pressure to control both air and fuel flow. Two main elements generate this differential pressure: the throttle plate and the venturi. Also used are ports, orifices and metering jets. Most carburetors use a second movable plate, called a choke. In addition to differential pressure controls, fuel level within the carburetor is limited by a float valve.

## Throttle Plate

The throttle plate is the butterfly valve connected to the throttle control. As the engine turns over, atmospheric pressure pushes air in through the carburetor, with the position of the throttle plate controlling how much air gets in. Unless the throttle is fully open, the plate causes some lowering of pressure in the areas downstream.

## Float Valve

One of the things that regulates fuel flow in the carburetor is the depth of the fuel in the carburetor float bowl. A consistent depth is maintained by the carburetor float valve. The float is a hollow brass pontoon hanging from a hinge on one end. As fuel from the tank flows in by gravity, the float raises on its hinge, actuating a needle valve, which shuts off further flow. Thus, other functions of the carburetor can rely on a regulated fuel level under all conditions.

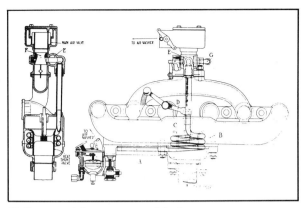

*Holley vaporizing system used for kerosene.*

## Venturi

The main barrel of the carburetor is slightly restricted by a streamlined sleeve called a venturi. This increases the air velocity, thereby lowering its pressure. Pressure drops even further as air velocity increases. This reduced pressure draws in the fuel through the main jet, proportional to air flow (engine speed).

## Main Jet

Fuel leaves the float chamber through a carefully sized passage known as the main jet, or metering jet, and into a passage called the metering well. This passage leads to the discharge nozzle protruding into the barrel at the smallest point of the venturi. The discharge nozzle is higher than the fuel level in the float chamber, so unless there is low pressure due to air flow, fuel flow stops. There is usually an adjustable air bleed port leading into the metering well to regulate the mixture ratio and to help atomize the fuel.

## Idle System

When the throttle is closed, there is too little air flow to create a low-pressure zone in the venturi. Therefore, the idle system picks up fuel in the metering well and injects it downstream of the throttle. Because the throttle is closed, this is an area of high vacuum. In the idle fuel passage, which is also routed above the float level to prevent continuous fuel flow when the engine is off, are bleed ports and an idle mixture screw. These break the siphoning effect and draw in air to make the idle mixture leaner.

## Choke

This butterfly valve is located upstream of the rest of the carburetor components mentioned. When closed, it creates enough vacuum to draw out the fuel necessary for starting. This also results in a much richer mixture, which aids in starting a cold engine.

## Fuel Tank Restoration

You probably removed the fuel tank when you stripped off the sheet metal to gain access to the engine. Thoroughly inspect it for dirt, leaks and rust. Remember, an apparently empty fuel tank can still contain explosive vapors, so check for leaks by either filling the tank with water and searching for drips, or pressurizing the tank with air and holding as much of it as you can under water and looking for bubbles. Don't allow much pressure to build, as the tank can be easily ruptured. Put your air hose nozzle in the tank opening and stuff some rags around it. If there is a separate tank vent, you will lose some air through it, but probably not too much. That will also be a

*Once the gas tank is removed for better access to the engine, a temporary tank must be provided to run the engine. This Ford-Ferguson 2N has such a tank attached to the cowl, with a copper tube running to the carburetor.*

good check to be sure the vent isn't restricted. Leaks can be repaired by a qualified welder or by purchased fuel tank sealants. I have even sealed a particularly stubborn leak with epoxy. The Eastwood Company (see the Sources section) sells gas tank etch to remove rust and a gas tank sealer.

If sediment, sludge or any other contamination is found in the tank, remove it with the steam jenny. If that is not convenient, try adding a gallon of water and a quart or two of pea gravel. Put on the cap and shake it vigorously for a few minutes. Then pour the whole mess out and let it dry. Before reinstallation, give it a coat of rust-resistant primer. If it's on the outside, you can paint over it when you paint the rest of the tractor; if it's under the hood, paint it before putting the hood back on.

Always check for proper and adequate tank venting. I would go so far as to contact the club or newsletter for the brand to see whether any safety bulletins have been issued. There have been several cases where engine heat has boiled the fuel in the tank mounted directly above it, and tank venting was not adequate to take care of the expansion. As a result, the tanks ruptured, burning the operators. I once found the fuel boiling in the tank of my 2N Ford-Ferguson, due to a slipping fan belt! Thank God for an adequate vent.

Fuel lines and strainer/sediment bowls are straightforward components. To solve any problems with them, it's best to simply replace them.

## Carburetor Restoration

Carburetors should be cleaned by soaking them in solvent, and unless they are functioning perfectly, they should have a rebuild kit incorporated. This may be a problem for older and orphan tractors. If you are not an experienced carburetor person, it may be best to acquire the services of a specialist.

Most vintage tractors use oil-bath air cleaners, which need to be removed and thoroughly cleaned. Flexible piping should be replaced, and any other sources of leaks should be plugged. Be sure to service this cleaner before putting the tractor to work.

Another often-overlooked part of the system is the intake manifold. Any leaks will reduce the carburetor vacuum and prevent proper operation. Look for gasket leaks and rust-through spots. These are also a source for dirt entering downstream of the air filter.

## Project Tractors

Both the Ford-Ferguson and Farmall A received carburetor overhauls. No other fuel system problems were uncovered.

*Chapter 6*

# Diesel Fuel Systems

The diesel engine is a compression-ignition type, as opposed to a spark-ignition engine. This means that the fuel, when injected into the combustion chamber, ignites solely due to the heat of the compressed air in the chamber. The advantages of the diesel engine are in fuel economy and in the characteristic torque curve, which is flatter than for most spark-ignition engines.

Disadvantages of the diesel engine are in its weight, cost and the critical requirements of some of its components.

### Diesel Development

The first diesel tractor tested at the University of Nebraska was the Caterpillar Diesel 65. The year was 1932. It was offered for sale to the public in October of that year, the first diesel tractor on the US market. The Caterpillar 65, a crawler, had a four-cylinder, four-cycle engine, which was governed at 650 rpm.

The first wheel-type diesel tractor was the famous McCormick Deering WD-40, introduced in 1934. It was a four-cylinder machine with about 50 belt horsepower. Because of its historical significance, it is a highly collectible specimen (not quite as prized as its industrial counterpart, the ID-40, however, as there were only 238 made).

The diesel engine was invented and initially produced by Dr. Rudolf Diesel, born in Paris of German parents in 1858. He obtained a patent on the compression-ignition principle in 1892 and built his first engine in 1893. The engine proved his theory of compression ignition, but it exploded and almost killed him.

By 1897, Diesel had perfected the engine to the point where it was commercially viable. Later, Sir Dugald Clerk of Great Britain developed the valve-less, two-cycle diesel. Since these are not likely to be found in tractors of the type we are interested in, we will cover only the four-cycle variety here.

### Diesel Fuel

Alternately called "diesel," "Number 2 fuel oil" or "distillate," diesel fuel is much like kerosene, jet fuel or heating oil. Originally, these fuels were much cheaper than gasoline, because the processing was less complicated. Distillates are made from the same parts of crude oil as gasoline, though, so competition for the limited resource has driven the price up to where, in many cases, diesel fuel costs more than gasoline. Diesels have lower fuel costs than a comparable spark-ignition engine, because of higher thermal and volumetric efficiency.

Factors contributing to higher thermal efficiency are the higher compression ratio (often, 22.0:1 or higher), better vaporization with the direct fuel injection and the lean mixture ratio (diesels normally operate on the lean side of the stoichiometric). Higher volumetric efficiency is the result of not having a carburetor, and its attendant throttle, in the air intake stream.

The major property requirement of diesel fuel is a factor called "ignition quality." As its name implies, ignition quality is a measure of the ease with which the fuel can be ignited. This affects cold starting, combustion roughness, smoke and combustion-chamber deposits.

Ignition quality also affects the length of the "delay period," or the time between the initiation of

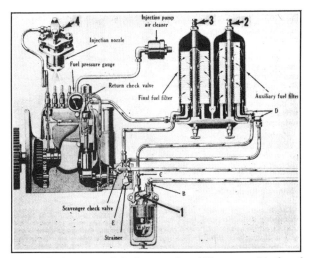

*Diesel fuel system of the International Harvester M, 6 and 9 Series. The components are typical of most diesel systems.* Intertec

injection and the beginning of combustion. Combustion chamber turbulence and injector nozzle spray pattern also influence the delay period.

Diesel fuel ignition quality is measured by its "cetane rating," which is established in a test engine much like octane ratings are determined for gasoline. High cetane-rated fuels have good ignition quality and low auto-ignition temperatures.

Three basic units compose a diesel fuel system: fuel filters, injection pump and injection nozzles.

## Filters

A typical fuel-filtering system consists of a water trap and two cartridge filters. Some also include a sediment bowl and more filtration stages because diesel fuel systems cannot tolerate even minute traces of foreign particles.

## Injection Pump

An injection pump forces an exact amount of fuel through the injector and into the combustion chamber at precisely the right time. Thus, it controls the amount of power produced and the ignition timing. You will find two main types of pumps: the in-line multiplunger pump, with a plunger for each cylinder; and the distributor, or Stanadyne pump, which uses only one plunger and a distribution block. Most have a feed pump element integrated with the injection pump to ensure that the plunger cylinder fills properly on the intake stroke. Some also have a scavenger element to return excess fuel to the inlet.

The injection pump is geared to the crankshaft, both to provide for its driving power and to affect the timing function. Power (throttle) is controlled by varying the displacement of the injector pump according to the position of the throttle lever. Since the air intake is never restricted on a diesel, the term "throttle" is somewhat of a misnomer; the proper term is probably "power lever."

Nevertheless, fuel inflow and, hence, power are controlled by rotating the pump plunger barrel. This

*The John Deere 830, as well as some of the other larger John Deere two-cylinder tractors, uses a four-cylinder pony motor for starting.*

alters port position, which changes the effective displacement of the injector pump.

## Fuel Injectors

The fuel injector, or spray nozzle, serves two principal functions: It atomizes the fuel and distributes it evenly throughout the combustion chamber. In some systems, it also plays a part in metering the fuel.

There are three basic types of nozzles: open nozzles that have no moving parts; nozzles that have valves, which are opened by fuel pressure; and nozzles that incorporate a cam mechanism to open their valves during injection of the fuel. In all cases, the nozzle is an important element, since the spray pattern produced is critical to proper diesel operation.

## Diesel Operation

A typical diesel engine, with a compression ratio of 22.0:1, must have a combustion-chamber pressure of around 500 pounds and a temperature near 1,000 degrees Fahrenheit before fuel is introduced by the injectors. Ignition takes place when the fuel, with a flash point of around 350 degrees Fahrenheit, meets the super-heated air.

The diesel engine is at its leanest mixture when idling. As injector pump displacement increases when the power lever is advanced, the fuel mixture becomes richer. Since there is no throttle on the diesel engine, the cylinders take in the same amount of air with each intake stroke. So, theoretically, regardless of engine speed or load, it takes the same volume of air with each revolution. In practice, however, losses in volumetric efficiency increase as speed increases. Thus, the supercharger, or turbocharger, is a great boon to the diesel, since it overcomes such losses and either makes the mixture leaner or allows more fuel at high-power outputs. At full power, or when the power lever is sharply advanced, the diesel can cross from the lean side of stoichiometric to the rich side—emitting black smoke from the exhaust.

Diesel combustion occurs in four steps. When first injected, there is a delay period as the fuel changes from an atomized liquid to a vapor. This is followed by an uncontrolled period when the excess fuel injected during the delay period flashes. Next is the controlled period. Once the fire is started, continued injection results in smooth, even burning and expansion. This period is timed to occur as the piston rises over top dead center and starts down on the power stroke. When the piston has traveled to the point where all useful expansion has taken place, injection stops. Fuel already in the chamber continues to burn, however, in what is called the afterburn period.

The injection system is the critical part of the diesel engine, but it is not to be confused with gasoline-engine fuel-injection systems. Diesel injector pumps often develop 30,000 psi, and the tubing

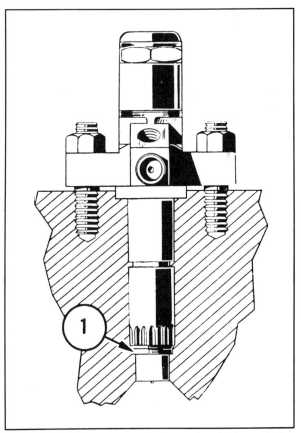

*Sectional view of an Allis-Chalmers diesel injector. When rebuilding the injectors, always replace the copper gasket (1). Intertec*

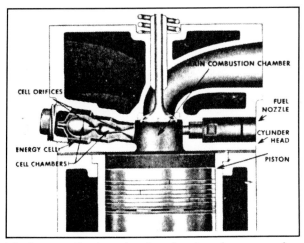

*The Lanova diesel combustion chamber, the type used on early Oliver tractors.*

between the injector pump and the injector has to be robust to handle such tremendous pulsating pressures. Furthermore, each tube has to be the same length as all others so that tube expansion and hydraulic modulus will be the same for each cylinder, assuring the same amount of fuel to each. (If you ever are checking the spray pattern of an injector nozzle, be sure that it isn't pointing at you or anything else that you don't want penetrated.)

Since the volume of fuel handled on each injection is extremely small, just a tiny particle of foreign matter can plug up the works. Injection pump plungers, for example, are lapped to fit the barrel with just enough clearance so that some fuel can leak through to provide lubrication. If that leakage is prevented by

contamination, the injector pump will wear rapidly. Anyone who uses hair spray will know what happens to the spray pattern when the nozzle becomes plugged. Just the slightest alteration from the ideal pattern in a diesel engine will make for a rough ride, or even no operation at all.

In addition to no particle contamination, there must be no air in the diesel fuel system. The slightest amount of air can prevent the system from hydraulically functioning. It is just like having air in a hydraulic brake system. The air, which has a high capability for expansion and contraction, absorbs the output of the injector pump, preventing the build-up of pressure. Most injectors have facilities for easy bleeding of the system should air get in, such as when the filters are changed.

## Troubleshooting

If the engine is missing, you should be able to determine which cylinder is not firing by momentarily opening the bleed port for each cylinder, one at a time, until you find the cylinder or cylinders least affected by the open bleed port.

Most repairs or rebuilding of diesel fuel system components require specialized equipment. For example, a flow bench measures injector pump output at different operating speeds, and accurate flow/pressure measuring equipment determines whether internal leakage rates are within tolerance.

The *I&T Shop Service Manual* will have specific troubleshooting procedures for your brand of tractor.

---

### Diesel Troubleshooting Checklist

When troubleshooting your tractor's diesel fuel system, here are some of the first items to inspect:
- Water or dirt in the fuel
- Air in the system
- Leaking or clogged fuel lines
- Clogged filters or water trap
- Wrong fuel
- Improperly timed injection pump
- Defective or plugged nozzle
- Sticking injection pump plunger
- Scored or dirty injection pump plunger
- Faulty distributor block
- Faulty charge or scavenger pumps

---

# Chapter 7

# Governor Rebuilding

Steam engine and tractor operators enjoyed the benefits of governed speed control, but the earliest internal-combustion engine tractors relied on the operator to adjust the throttle according to the load. These early tractors were single-cylinder types. They were first fitted with hit-or-miss governors developed for similar stationary engines.

## Governor Types

With the hit-or-miss type of governor, engine speed fluctuates widely, making them somewhat unsuited for belt work, at least compared to the steady-running steam engine.

When the engine is above its nominal speed, the governor causes the exhaust valve to be held open and the intake valve closed, so it does not receive a charge. When the engine gets below the nominal speed, the governor releases the valves to function normally.

The advent of the multi-cylinder tractor in about 1910 also saw the development of throttle governors. Most tractors from that time on had

*The governor of the Farmall A. This unit did not require rebuilding. Only some readjustment was required.*

governors that adjusted the throttle to hold working engine speed. Later, in the thirties and after, most governors were of the variable-speed type, and would regulate the speed around the set point determined by the throttle lever position.

There are a variety of brand-name governors used by tractor manufacturers over the years; brands such as Pierce and Pickering were common in the twenties. The Ford and Ford-Ferguson tractors used a governor, the mechanism of which was provided by

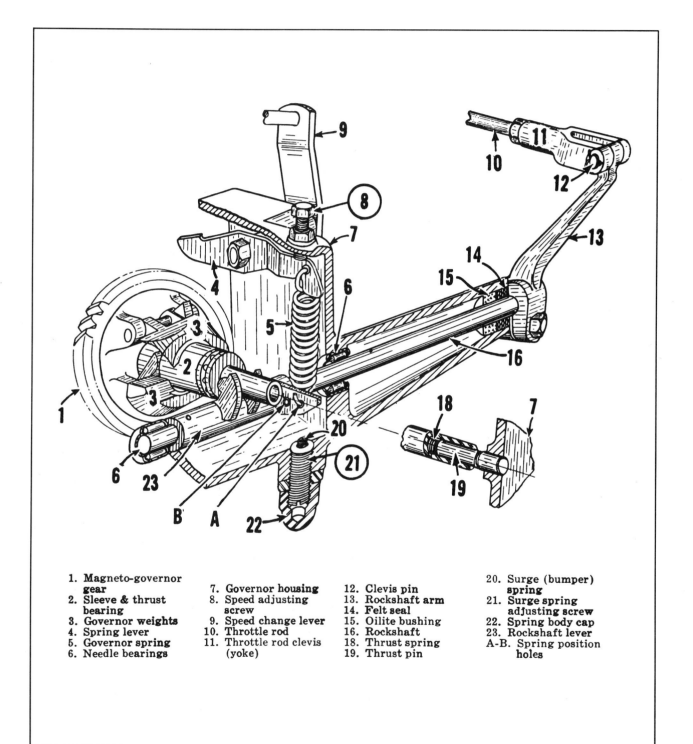

1. Magneto-governor gear
2. Sleeve & thrust bearing
3. Governor weights
4. Spring lever
5. Governor spring
6. Needle bearings
7. Governor housing
8. Speed adjusting screw
9. Speed change lever
10. Throttle rod
11. Throttle rod clevis (yoke)
12. Clevis pin
13. Rockshaft arm
14. Felt seal
15. Oilite bushing
16. Rockshaft
18. Thrust spring
19. Thrust pin
20. Surge (bumper) spring
21. Surge spring adjusting screw
22. Spring body cap
23. Rockshaft lever
A-B. Spring position holes

*Cutaway view of the Farmall A, B and C series governor.*
Intertec

Novi Engineering. Other tractor makers designed their own governing devices. Most were driven by the magneto, distributor or timing gear.

Diesel governors are part of the injector assembly. They function on the same fly-weight system as carburetor governors, but limit the stroke of the injector pump to the volume of fuel that will produce the desired speed.

## Troubleshooting

When test driving your tractor, you can load the engine by driving up a grade in a higher gear with part throttle. When engine load reaches the point where speed begins to fall off, move the throttle lever to the full-open position. If more power is evident, the governor is not working properly. A properly functioning governor would have already had the throttle butterfly all the way open.

Other signs of a malfunctioning governor include the engine not idling down when the throttle lever is moved to the idle position, surging, over-revving and delayed reaction to changing load conditions.

With tractors of the late thirties and newer, governors are in most cases readily repairable. The

*I&T Shop Service Manual* for your tractor will have cutaway views and directions for repair. There are also places that specialize in rebuilding governors. Since the governor is such an important part of a tractor's function, replacing it with a rebuilt unit during restoration makes a lot of sense. See the Sources section for names and addresses.

## Project Tractors

The Ford-Ferguson 9N needed governor work. It was not correcting for load changes, and throttle lever response was erratic. The Novi governor used on these tractors employs a four-ball mechanism, running in a toroid on one side and a flat plate on the other. As speed increases toward the set point, the balls move outward, forcing the toroid away from the flat plate. This action moves a servo mechanism, which adjusts the throttle butterfly.

Tractors of serial number 357's vintage (before the mid-forties) did not have pressure lubrication for the governor. Serial number 357 now, however, was found to have an 8N governor with the lube line added.

When the governor of serial number 357 was disassembled, it was found that the balls had worn

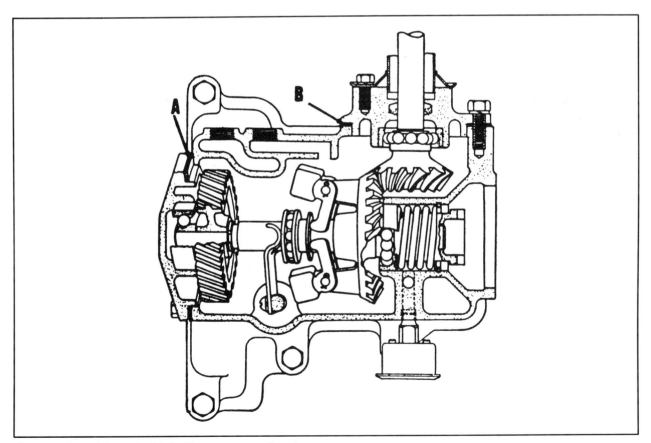

*Cutaway view of the typical John Deere governor.* Intertec

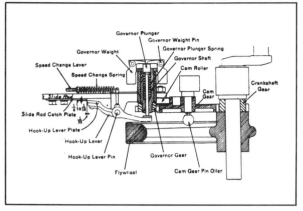

*Hit-and-miss governor.*

grooves in the toroid and plate at the position corresponding to normal working speed. Thus, the balls got hung up in the grooves and could not respond until the speed was quite far from the set point.

After seeing the condition of serial number 357's governor, and since it was not of the right configuration, Fossum replaced it with a proper cast-iron housing with new insides. He had his cousin, Vernon Fossum (also of Northfield, Minnesota, and owner of a business rebuilding Ford 9N, 2N and 8N governors and linkages) rebuild the throttle-governor linkage for serial number 357.

It is interesting to note that, in the interest of authentic originality, Palmer Fossum removed the governor pressure lube line and replaced the line going to the oil filter as it originally was. In doing so, he discovered that the oil filter housing also was of a later configuration; 1939 filter housings have smooth bottoms, while later ones have reinforcing flutes. He got an original configuration housing from another 1939 tractor he had, but found that the threads of the hole for the brass drain plug had been stripped. It was a simple matter to retap the hole, but now a standard plug would not fit, so a machinist customized a plug with a standard-size head on a larger-than-standard body. Thus, serial number 357 is restored to original appearance.

The Farmall A governor seemed to work quite well, so it was not removed. When the engine was completely overhauled and the initial run in had taken place, Joe Schloskey set low idle, high idle and no-load speeds. These adjustments are made with the engine stopped by adjusting the linkage to assure full throttle butterfly travel. When the engine was again run, some surging was noticed. This was corrected by adjusting the bumper, or surge, spring until the tendency to surge was eliminated.

# Chapter 8

# Air, Water and Oil Cooling Systems

We must deal with engine heat, because engines are less than one-hundred percent efficient. Both combustion efficiency (the conversion of the thermal energy of the fuel to work) and mechanical efficiency (the theoretical output of the engine versus the actual output) are less than one-hundred percent. The fraction of efficiency that is lost produces heat. A British Thermal Unit (Btu) is the amount of heat required to raise the temperature of one pound of water 1 degree Fahrenheit. There are 42.42 Btu per

horsepower. Therefore, if a tractor has losses equalling 10 horsepower, it has a cooling load of 424.2 Btu per minute—enough Btu to heat a small house.

## Styles of Cooling Systems

Over the years, quite a few systems have been tried to best dissipate this cooling load to the

*An 8N type radiator, as found on serial number 357. For a work tractor restoration, this would have been better than the original, since it uses a pressure cap. For a parade tractor, however, the correct radiator for the period had to be installed.*

*The correct radiator for Ford-Ferguson serial number 357 after its return from the radiator shop.*

surrounding atmosphere. Both air cooling and liquid cooling schemes have been tried. Of course, liquid cooling systems are ultimately cooled by air, but for the sake of discussion, we will refer to them simply as air or liquid cooling systems.

Air cooling found most of its adherents in the aircraft business, rather than in the tractor business. I suppose it is obvious: Airplanes go quickly; tractors go slowly and therefore, don't get much free airflow. Nevertheless, there have been adherents to the principle of air cooling for tractor and stationary engines, mainly by the German Deutz company. The main advantage of air cooling is the unlimited supply of coolant, which you do not have to carry with you. The main disadvantage is the amount of power required to force this air through the engine's cooling passages.

The main advantage of liquid cooling is the physical principle known as the "latent heat of vaporization." The Btu input required to raise a liquid's temperature is constant per degree of rise, until the boiling temperature is reached. At this point, additional heat does not raise the temperature, but causes some of the liquid to evaporate. As long as it stays a liquid, the liquid's temperature cannot exceed its boiling temperature. The amount of Btu required to boil it away greatly exceeds that required to merely raise the temperature to the boiling point.

Thus, the job of the liquid-cooled engine designer is simplified, because the temperature range of the liquid is predictable, and generally, quite constant, if a thermostat is used.

Early tractors simply boiled away a tank of water while they worked, without trying to cool the liquid in the reservoir. That meant stopping to refill every few hours. Open recirculating systems were added, along with some kind of a pump. The coolant was sometimes allowed to flow down a cooling screen to increase the heat exchange rate.

Next came closed-loop systems, with induced cooling by means of the cooling tower effect. The liquid—water or oil—was circulated through coils in a stack, which was open at the bottom and top. Air was expected to go in the bottom and rise out the top as it picked up heat. Now, designers took a tip from the steam engine. The steam engine induces draft for the firebox by exhausting steam up the stack; kerosene engine tractors did a like thing with their exhaust, causing the stack to draw more air flow.

Many early tractors were of the "cross-motor," or transverse, configuration, which allowed power to be transferred to the drive wheels, or wheel, by straight spur gearing. This meant that driving a radiator fan was not as straightforward as if the engine were mounted longitudinally. The radiator and fan were usually mounted crosswise as well. Nevertheless, conventional fan/radiator systems were somewhat slower in coming to cross-motor tractors.

Some early tractors, such as the Fordson, John Deere and early Farmalls (including the Farmall A being restored for this book), used a thermosyphon circulating system. Hot water, being lighter, was forced upward through the radiator by the heavier cold water, thus inducing cooling circulation. Centrifugal pumps, however, soon became the norm for tractors, just as for automobiles.

In the days before commercial antifreeze solutions, such as Prestone, became available, farmers had to drain the water from the radiators and blocks of

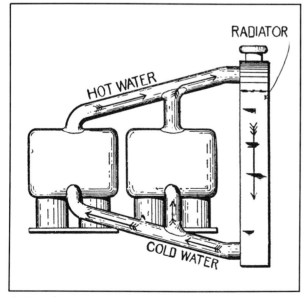

*Action of a simple thermo-siphon cooling system.*

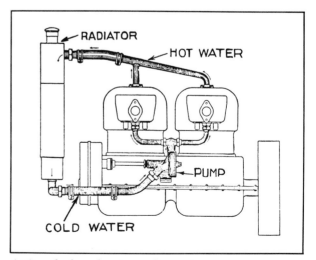

*Action of a forced-water cooling system.*

their tractors whenever a long period of shutdown was anticipated during freezing weather. Needless to say, this was an inconvenience. Water-alcohol mixtures worked well enough in automobiles, but the alcohol lowered the boiling point of the mixture to where it did not work well in most tractors. Some of the more enterprising of the early tractor pioneers switched from water to a light oil as a coolant. Their reasoning was that leaks into the combustion chamber and crankcase were not too detrimental with the oil coolant; hence, the several "Oil-Pull" tractors.

It is interesting to note that Adiabatics Incorporated, Columbus, Indiana, is trying to develop engine coatings and treatments that allow engines to run without cooling systems. Indeed, their efforts are to contain the heat generated and to use it to produce power, instead of using more fuel for that purpose. This company has had quite good success with both gasoline and diesel engines. The military is interested in these developments, because radiators are so vulnerable on battle vehicles.

## Restoring Cooling Systems

We will concentrate on conventional liquid cooling systems, which include a radiator and cap, fan and fan belt, pump, thermostat, temperature gauge, hoses and engine passages.

If you were able to test drive your tractor before you brought it home, you probably saw the action of the temperature gauge (if so equipped). If the temperature of the coolant came up to mid-range and stabilized, you had every reason to gain confidence. If you then found no oil in the water, nor water in the oil, your confidence in the state of the cooling system could be fairly secure. One final check: Any visual evidence of leaks? If not, you have a system that will give you good service—providing you don't create some leaks while you're doing the rest of the restoration.

If you were unable to gain confidence in the tractor's cooling system but bought it anyway, you must isolate the offending components and get them repaired.

## Radiator

Wet spots on the radiator core, or puddles beneath, indicate leaks. If the leaks are minor, radiator stop-leak compound will likely solve your problem. Be sure to follow the manufacturer's directions, however. If there are visible cracks, holes, split seams, or the like, you may as well pull the radiator and take it to a radiator shop.

Most tractor radiators can be pulled quite easily, and should be pulled periodically for access to the

engine, and the radiator should be taken in for flushing and checking, even if there are no indications of trouble. By the time you are ready for it, it will be in first-class condition, ready for fifty more years of service.

## Radiator Cap

In the early forties, most tractor makers adopted pressurized cooling systems. This means that the radiator cap had a built-in pressure-regulating system that could raise the pressure in the cooling system due to expansion from the heat by as much as 15 psi. Raising the pressure raises the boiling point, which allows the use of a higher-temperature thermostat, which is better for the engine. It also makes a radiator of a given size able to reject more heat, since the temperature differential between the coolant and the air is greater.

The relief setting for the cap should not be too high, or the radiator may be damaged. Also, never remove a pressure cap while the radiator is hot, as the coolant may flash to steam with scalding results. Instead, take the cap to a radiator shop and have it tested.

Neither the project Ford-Ferguson nor the Farmall A required radiator repair, other than flushing and painting. Neither was equipped with a pressure-type radiator cap.

## Cooling Fan

Not much can go wrong with a cooling fan, other than obviously bent or broken blades. If there is any evidence of the fan hitting the core of the radiator, check the fan for wobble or vibration. The problem could be in the fan bearings.

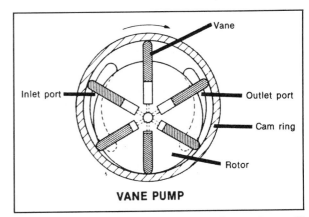

**VANE PUMP**

*The vane pump has five or more recessed vanes in an off-center rotor. Fluid is swept before the vanes from the inlet to the outlet. Centrifugal force and hydraulic pressure (entering through the axle) extend the vanes against the cam ring.*

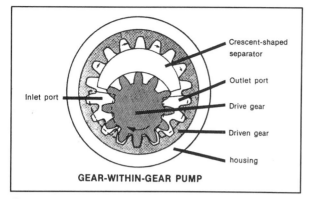

Gerotor, or gear-within-gear, pump. The small gear drives the larger gear, carrying the fluid around the outside of the crescent from the inlet to the outlet. The large gear slides within the housing on a film of hydraulic oil. A common variation of this design does not use the crescent separator, but instead, the small gear is sized to just clear the teeth of the large gear on the non-mesh side.

There are many different fan configurations for most tractors. If you are doing a show tractor, it will be important to determine its original configuration. The Ford-Ferguson had the wrong fan at the start of restoration. The earliest Ford-Fergusons had fans that blew through the radiator from back to front, not the best configuration. Palmer Fossum, the restorer, insisted that the correct fan for the serial number be found. He was lucky: A tractor buff named Clayton Risner, from Fostoria, Ohio, came to view Fossum's tractor collection. In the course of the tour, Fossum was explaining his need for a "backwards" fan, and Risner said he thought he might have one at home. A few days later, Fossum's mail contained the sought-after fan.

A fan shroud will greatly improve the cooling ability of the fan. Be sure that the corners of the shroud are not clogged with dirt and debris.

### Fan Belt

A loose or missing fan belt will debilitate a cooling system quicker than anything, because the belt also usually drives the water pump. If the belt isn't functioning properly, neither air nor water will flow.

To function properly, a V-belt type of fan belt must be wide enough not to bottom out in the pulley. The belt may seem to be tight enough and may appear to be in good condition, but its traction comes from the wedging action of the belt in the pulley. The belt may have been worn narrow from not being tight enough to prevent slippage. If in doubt, change it.

### Water Pump

To check the water pump for operation, look into the top of the radiator, with the cap removed, while the engine is idling. When the water gets warm enough to open the thermostat, you should begin to see it swirling in the upper tank area as it flows out of the upper radiator hose. If no flow is indicated and the drive belt and thermostat are functional, you may have worn or broken impeller blades. If this is the case, you may be able to have the blades welded back on (if you can find them) or have new blades welded on. If parts are readily available, such as for the Ford-Ferguson and Farmall A, you are far better off to replace the pump.

A common problem with water pumps is shaft seal leakage. For older tractors, you may find a string-type packing that was forced around the shaft where it entered the housing. You can get this packing from a plumbing shop and replace it in your

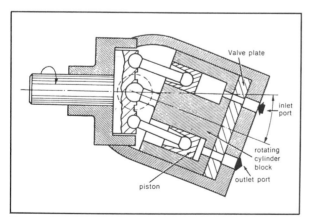

Bent-axis pump. The input shaft drives the piston block and pistons through a constant-velocity universal joint. The angle of the bend determines the piston stroke, so this type can readily be made variable-displacement.

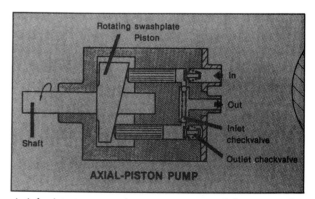

Axial piston pump pistons are actuated by a rotating swashplate. Charge pressure, pressurizing the inlet side of this type of pump, is necessary to force the pistons against the swashplate.

tractor without removing the pump. Newer pumps had washer-type shaft seals. To replace this kind of seal, you will have to remove the pump.

### Thermostat

If there was no indication of flow in the upper radiator tank when you checked for pump operation, the fault may be in the thermostat. The thermostat is usually on the engine-end of the upper radiator hose. Remove it and test it by putting it in a pan of boiling water; as the water gets hot, the spring should shrink and the diaphragm should open. If this does not happen, you need a new thermostat. If your tractor is an orphan, take the old thermostat to a NAPA parts supplier and see whether they can find one that will do the job.

It is possible to operate the tractor without a thermostat, but it won't do the engine any good. If a reliable temperature gauge is installed, you can use your tractor for light-duty operations by blocking part of the radiator to achieve the desired temperature. Many earlier tractors had shutters or a blind device over the radiator.

### Temperature Gauge

Not many old tractors had temperature gauges in their dashboards. Some had a direct-reading mercury thermometer protruding from the radiator cap, but on such tractors as the Ford-Ferguson and the Farmall A, the first indication of overheating was steam coming from the radiator cap.

Little can go wrong with the direct-reading thermometer. Just check that the tube on the bottom is clean and tight.

The electric temperature gauge also requires little service. If it doesn't work, check the wiring first. Sometimes, blocks, cylinder heads and radiators get so plugged with rusty sludge that the temperature sender is completely isolated. If this seems to be the problem, a complete flush job is in order.

If the gauge is faded or broken, and you are restoring a tractor for show you will need the services of a specialist. Check the Yellow Pages under "Automotive Electrics" or "Automobile, Antiques."

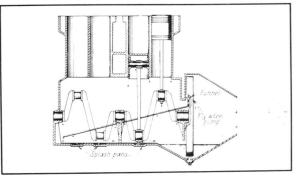

*Splash-type lubrication system where the crankshaft is relied on to circulate oil.*

### Radiator Hoses

It almost goes without saying that you should never put your tractor back together without replacing the hoses. If you are doing a show tractor, you cannot use the readily available universal hose, because it isn't original equipment. Most tractor hoses are rather simple, and for more complex variations, you should be able to find something fairly close at your local parts store. Also don't overlook the necessity of having the correct hose clamps for your vintage show tractor.

### Freeze Plugs

Most engines have one or more round holes in the block casting, with thin sheet-metal plugs pressed in. It was expected that in the event of a freeze-up, the expansion would be taken up by forcing these plugs out. Then, it would be a simple matter to pound in some new plugs or even the old ones if they were not distorted. In practice, the plugs do get forced out, but the block usually cracks, too. In actual fact, the holes are required by the foundry to get the casting sand out.

Nevertheless, if your tractor has freeze plugs, be sure they are not rusted or distorted, as they are much easier to replace while the tractor is stripped down.

The 1939 version of the Ford-Ferguson 9N, such as serial number 357, had only one freeze plug on the back of the block. More were added to the 1940 and subsequent models.

# Chapter 9

# Ignition and Electrical Systems

Most people undertaking the restoration of a tractor will have a fairly good understanding of automotive electrical technology, but for the sake of those who don't and to standardize the usage of terms, let us begin with a discussion of electrical basics. If you've read the chapter on hydraulics, you'll recognize many similarities between hydraulic and electrical systems. The main difference is that hydraulic leaks cause puddles and electrical leaks cause fires.

Many early tractors had no electrical system, except for magneto ignition. Even for those that had a

starter, lights, panel instruments and so on, the systems are not complex. But first, the terms, definitions and descriptions of components.

## Voltage

This is the standard unit of electromotive force. Voltage is the electrical equivalent to pressure in the hydraulic system. The higher the voltage, the smaller the wires that can be used for a given task—just as smaller tubing can be used in a high-pressure hydraulic system.

*The electrical system of the Farmall A was marginal as originally designed, and a former owner of this one had made some revisions. As shown in this view, a voltage regulator from a car has been installed and haphazardly wired to the automotive six-volt generator. Joe Schloskey replaced it all with a modern twelve-volt alternator system.*

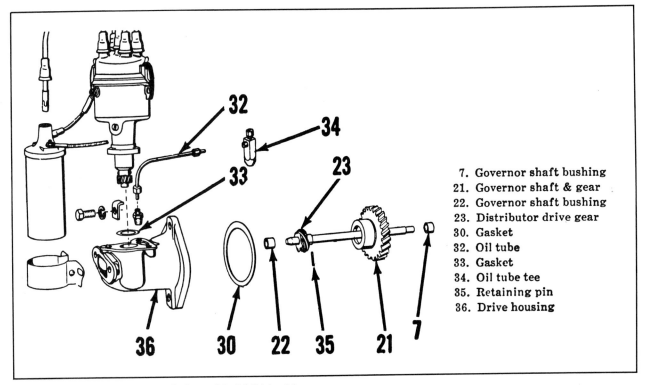

7. Governor shaft bushing
21. Governor shaft & gear
22. Governor shaft bushing
23. Distributor drive gear
30. Gasket
32. Oil tube
33. Gasket
34. Oil tube tee
35. Retaining pin
36. Drive housing

*An exploded view of the Allis-Chalmers Model CA ignition system.* Intertec

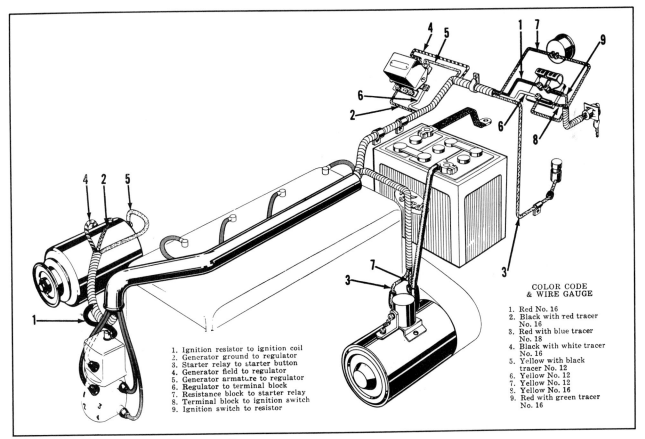

1. Ignition resistor to ignition coil
2. Generator ground to regulator
3. Starter relay to starter button
4. Generator field to regulator
5. Generator armature to regulator
6. Regulator to terminal block
7. Resistance block to starter relay
8. Terminal block to ignition switch
9. Ignition switch to resistor

COLOR CODE
& WIRE GAUGE

1. Red No. 16
2. Black with red tracer No. 16
3. Red with blue tracer No. 18
4. Black with white tracer No. 16
5. Yellow with black tracer No. 12
6. Yellow No. 12
7. Yellow No. 12
8. Yellow No. 16
9. Red with green tracer No. 16

*Electrical system used on Ford 8N tractor.* Intertec

## Amps

This is the amount of electricity flowing in the circuit. Amps times volts equals watts, the unit of electrical power. Thus, the same amount of power is produced in a six-volt system at ten amps as in a twelve-volt system at five amps.

## Electrical Circuits

Just as in a hydraulic system, electricity flows from its source (the battery) to the load (starter, lights and so on) and back to the source. A hydraulic circuit will provide power for a while without a return (until the fluid runs out), but an electrical circuit will not.

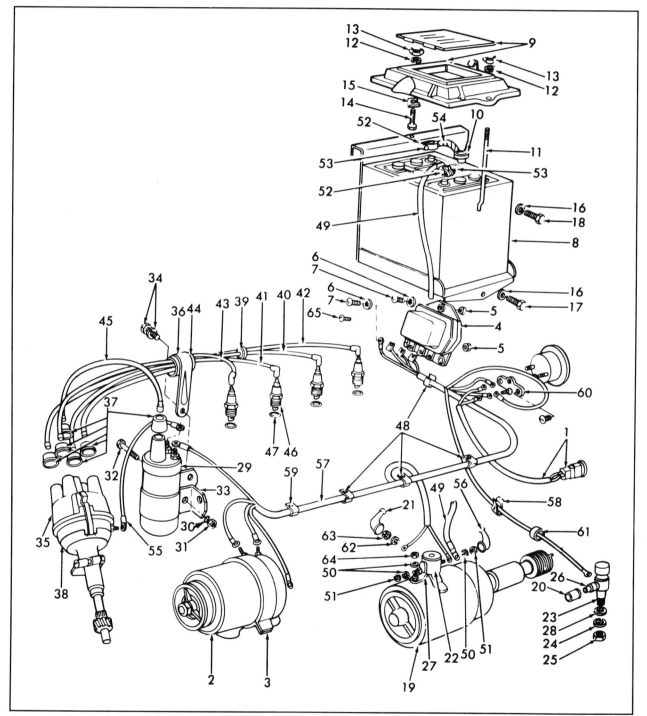

*A tractor electrical system, here from an N Series Ford, showing the generator (2), the battery (52), the starter (19),* *the voltage regulator (4), the coil (29), and the distributor (38).*

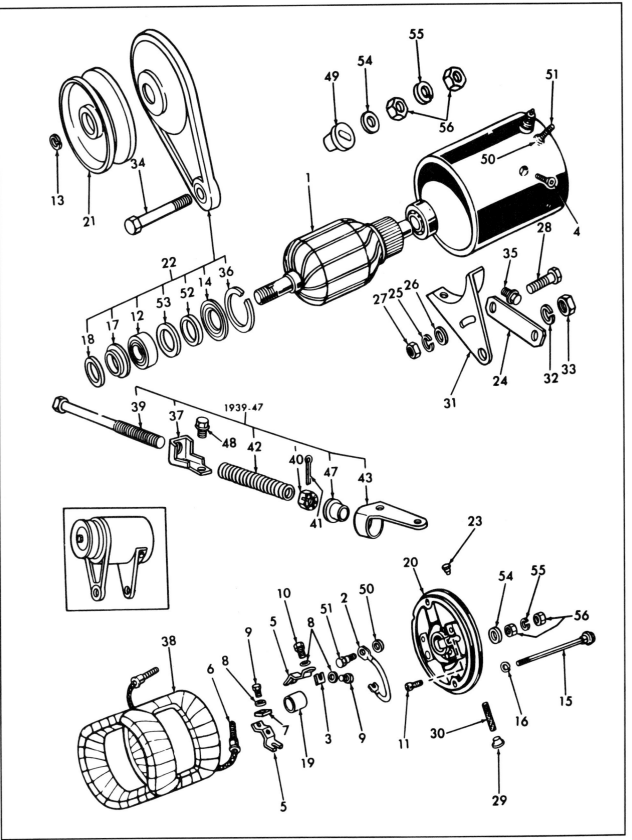

*A typical three-brush generator. The armature (1) rotates inside the field coil (38). Power is taken from the armature by brushes (7), which ride on the commutator, the smaller straight section on the end of the armature.*

There have been questions over the years as to which way the electricity flowed: positive to negative, or the other way around. In actual practice (until electronics are involved), it doesn't make much difference. Nevertheless, electrical circuits, like magnets, are polarized. Rather than define the poles as "north" and "south," as with magnets, "positive" and "negative" are used.

Originally, circuits were for one element only, such as a self-starter. Heavy wires ran from the battery, to a switch, to the starter, and back to the battery. As more items were added to the load, the return wire was eliminated and the frame of the vehicle was used instead. Thus, one terminal of the battery and of each load item are attached to the chassis, frame or, in the case of most tractors, to cast iron. This is referred to as being "grounded."

As stated earlier, it makes no difference whether the positive or the negative is used as the return (grounded to the frame), but one must be consistent. The path to the load must always be "above ground," and the return must be grounded. Many older tractors, up to the mid-forties, used a positive ground system. After that time, the conventional began to change to negative ground.

## Battery

Technically, a storage battery is a reservoir for electricity. Its counterpart in hydraulics would be the accumulator. Batteries have two posts, or terminals: The one marked with a plus sign is the positive terminal and the other, marked with a minus sign, is the negative terminal. If the positive terminal of the battery is grounded, the positive pole of the generator will also be grounded.

The battery is really a source of chemical energy. It consists of several lead plate cells connected internally to add their outputs (connected in series). Each cell is filled with a solution of sulfuric acid and water. When a load is put on the battery, the acid combines with the lead to make lead sulfate and, in the process, releases ionized particles that migrate to the opposite polarity plate, thereby creating an electrical potential, or voltage.

Each cell is sized to produce two volts. A six-volt battery, most common in the tractors we are likely to encounter, has three such cells. A twelve-volt battery, such as is found in some early diesel tractors and in more modern cars, trucks and tractors, will have six cells. There will be one water-fill cap for each cell.

If the load is kept on the battery long enough, too much of the sulfuric acid is converted to lead

sulfate for the process to continue, and voltage begins to fall off rapidly.

When the battery is charged (that is, refilled), the process is reversed. Lead sulfate is ionized at the high-voltage plate, forming sulfuric acid and building up the potential of the opposite plate. Eventually, the capability of the plates to perform their chemical function deteriorates, and the battery is no longer useful. It should be noted that for the battery to receive a charge, the input voltage must be higher than the battery voltage. Thus, a generator in a six-volt system will produce seven or eight volts.

## Generator

The function of the generator is to replace in the battery the electrical energy used in the circuit. The generator is usually driven by a V-belt from a pulley on the front of the engine.

The two main parts on a generator are the armature and the field. The field is electromagnetized by power from the battery. The armature, in the standard case, rotates within the field, cutting lines of magnetic flux produced by the field, and building up within itself an electric potential (voltage). This voltage is removed from the rotating armature, called the rotor, via carbon brushes (carbon terminals that ride on the armature, conducting the electricity out of the rotating part of the stationary part).

There are two types of generators in use: the direct current (DC) generator and the alternating current (AC) type, commonly called an alternator. Generators are constructed in much the same way as electric motors, only in the case of the generator, the rotor is forced through the magnetic field, rather than being driven by it.

An alternator differs from a DC generator in that the armature portion is stationary, rather than the rotating part, and the field portion rotates in the center. This eliminates the need for the power produced to exit via carbon brushes, which have always been the weak point of the DC generator.

In most DC versions, three brushes ride on the commutator: One delivers the current to the circuit, one is grounded, and one is adjusted to provide the desired current level. The commutator is a segmented portion of the rotor shaft, with each segment connected electrically to an arm of the armature. As the armature rotates through the lines of magnetic flux, only one polarity of electromotive force is connected by the commutator to the outside. Therefore, the generator produces only the one polarity of voltage.

The alternator uses three separate armature windings, or coils (which, in this case, are stationary). Normally, the rotating field is a multipoled rotor with twelve poles: six north poles and six south poles. The pole magnetism is electromagnetically induced through small slip rings, or brushes, which do not need to carry much power. Once induced, much of the power required to keep it energized is provided internally.

As the field rotates within the armature, both polarity lines of flux are cut; therefore, the output voltage changes polarity during each revolution. AC is changed to DC by a diode rectifier (the electrical equivalent of a check valve). Thus, the output of the alternator is DC. We cannot use AC as we do in our houses, because the frequency of an AC system depends on the speed of the alternator and, since electric motors, lights and so on need to receive power at a constant frequency, it would not work too well with the engine going up and down in speed. For house power, the commercial electric companies go to great lengths to see that their alternators run at exactly sixty hertz (cycles). Aircraft, which have used AC systems since about 1946, generally use a hydrostatic device made by the Sundstrand Corporation, known as a constant-speed drive, to change varying engine speeds to a constant output speed for the alternator. Constant-speed drives are, however, highly complex and sophisticated devices and cost about as much as a new tractor.

### Voltage Regulator

The function of the voltage regulator is to hold the generated voltage at the desired level for charging the battery. There are two types common in antique tractors: the cut-out and the vibrating type. The operation of the two is similar, but the vibrating type is more elaborate. A third type, a transistorized, or solid-state, regulator is used with alternators. Since these are not repairable, their function will not be described.

Each of the non-solid-state types contains, as its main functional part, an electromagnet switch. Voltage from the generator energizes the coil of this electromagnet switch and, as it exceeds the desired level, it breaks the contact connecting battery voltage to the generator field, allowing the field to decay.

In the vibrator regulator, current is still supplied to the field, but through a resistor that lowers the voltage. In either case, the amount of magnetism in the field is reduced and the generated voltage is lowered. When the generated voltage drops sufficiently, the electromagnet again closes the field contact, and the cycle is repeated. The cycles are repeated at sufficiently high frequency so that the voltage appears to be steady at the desired level. When the load current is high enough to lower battery voltage, regulator contacts remain closed and the generator maintains a charge rate limited by its capacity and speed.

Some older tractors, such as the International Harvester line, had two-position voltage regulator (cut-out) switches with which you could select one of two current levels. Thus, if the lights were being used, the higher level would be selected.

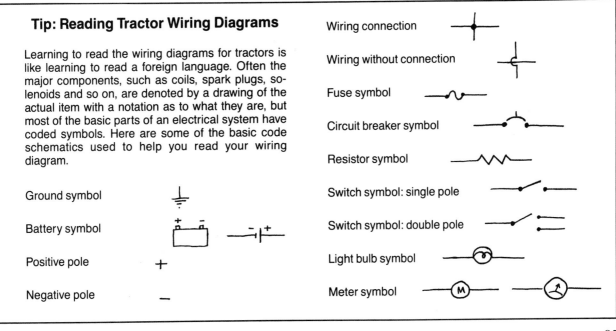

### Tip: Reading Tractor Wiring Diagrams

Learning to read the wiring diagrams for tractors is like learning to read a foreign language. Often the major components, such as coils, spark plugs, solenoids and so on, are denoted by a drawing of the actual item with a notation as to what they are, but most of the basic parts of an electrical system have coded symbols. Here are some of the basic code schematics used to help you read your wiring diagram.

Ground symbol

Battery symbol

Positive pole

Negative pole

Wiring connection

Wiring without connection

Fuse symbol

Circuit breaker symbol

Resistor symbol

Switch symbol: single pole

Switch symbol: double pole

Light bulb symbol

Meter symbol

### Current-Limiting Regulator

Usually in the same box as the voltage regulator, the current-limiting regulator functions in much the same way to prevent the generator from producing more current than its maximum safe output.

### Ammeter

The ammeter is the panel instrument that shows the amount of current flowing in the circuits. High-level, short-term power draws, like the starter circuit, are not connected through the ammeter. The function of the ammeter is to show whether the generator is keeping up with the power drain on the battery. Most ammeters are only graduated in degrees of "charge" or "discharge."

### Switches

Switches are the valves of the electrical system. They are installed downstream of the ammeter to turn the load on and off. The starter circuit does not go through the ammeter, because the amperage draw is so high that it would be way off scale. Generally, the ignition switch is operated by a key; in some later tractors, this switch acts as a master switch, controlling other circuits as well.

For the battery ignition system, the ignition switch connects power to the coil. For the magneto system, the ignition switch ungrounds the magneto for operation. For diesel tractors, the key switch often only enables the starter circuit. Once started, the key can be turned off and the tractor will remain running. These tractors have another means for stopping the engine: a stop-button switch, or manual lever, which shuts off the fuel supply.

Switching DC circuits is not an easy task, since the electricity will jump across the gap when the switch contacts approach one another. This is the same "arcing" process that occurs in an electric welder, when metal from one contact is carried by the arc to another. This arcing also takes place when the switch is opened. Thus, contacts of switches not properly designed for the application sometimes weld together, or build up peaks and pits that prevent them from carrying the current. Switch problems get worse as the voltage, or the current, goes up.

This is why six-volt systems were common for so many years, and twenty-four volts is the practical upper limit for automotive and aircraft DC systems. Modern aircraft use mostly AC systems, just as do commercial power companies, to avoid this switching problem. In AC systems, the voltage passes through zero at the beginning and at the middle of every cycle, the frequency of which is high enough to allow the switches to make and break without arcing.

Nevertheless, the starter switch is a critical component. There are two types: direct and solenoid. In the case of the direct, heavy switch contacts and a snap action are used to ensure that the contact is made as quickly and with as much surface area as possible. These switches are often mounted right on the starter and are operated by a linkage from the driver's seat.

The solenoid type is electrically actuated and also has a snap action and heavy contacts. When the starter button is pressed or the key switch is turned, current is directed to the coil of a relay, or solenoid, which magnetically snaps the contacts closed.

### Starter

The starter is a remarkably powerful electric motor designed for short-term duty. The drive mechanism, usually called the "Bendix," connects the starter to teeth on the engine flywheel. The flywheel gear is called the "ring gear." Since the ring gear is quite large in relation to the starter drive gear, a very high gear ratio is provided. Starter motors turn up to as much as 6,000 rpm to turn the engine at 200-300 rpm. When the engine fires and begins to accelerate, the starter must be disconnected, or it would be quickly driven to destruction. This, then, is the job of the Bendix drive.

To start the engine, the Bendix drive actuates automatically when the starter motor begins to turn—not by turning the drive gear, but by turning a threaded shaft inside the drive gear shaft, causing the drive gear to translate along the shaft until it meshes with the stationary flywheel ring gear. At this point, the internal shaft reaches the end of its threads and the drive gear begins to rotate, driving the ring gear.

When the engine fires and begins to run under its own power, it accelerates above starter speed, causing the starter gear to turn faster than the threaded internal shaft. This over-running action causes the internal shaft to withdraw the drive gear from the ring gear. A spring called the Bendix spring then completely backs the drive gear away from the ring gear and holds it in place for the next start.

### Primary and Secondary Circuits

The ignition system uses two separate electrical circuits: the primary of normal voltage, six or twelve volts (sometimes cut to a lower level by a resistor to protect the points), and the secondary of high voltage for the spark plugs, which can run as high as 20,000 volts.

### Coil

The coil is usually a cylindrical, beverage can-shaped item, mounted to the engine or firewall, or a

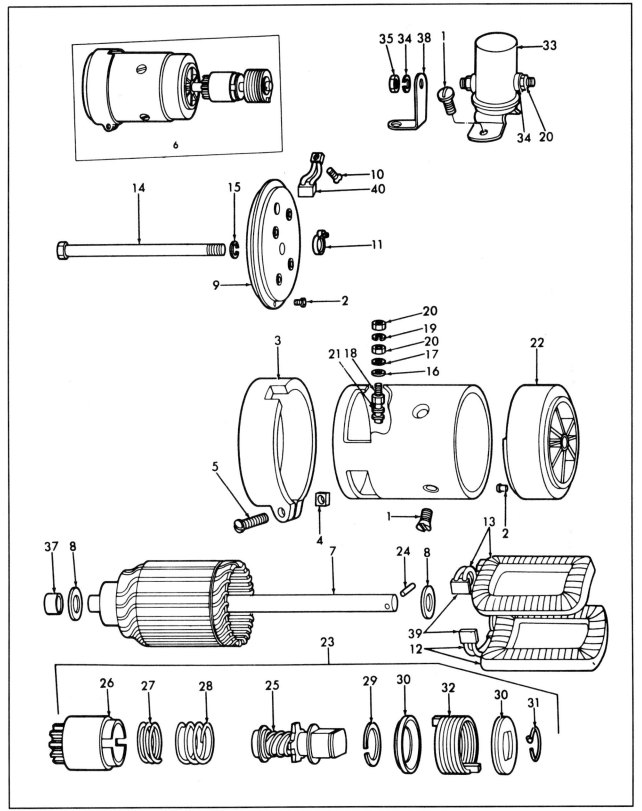

A starter motor with Bendix-type drive. The motor, built much like a generator with stator, armature, commutator and brushes, receives battery voltage via the solenoid (33). The Bendix mechanism causes the drive gear (26) to en-gage the engine flywheel before rotation begins. When the engine fires, causing the drive gear to go faster than the armature (7), the spiral teeth of (25) pull the drive gear out of mesh with the flywheel.

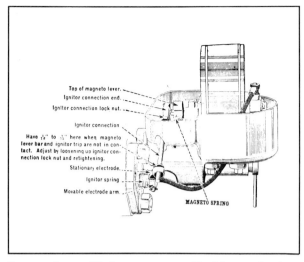

*Low-tension oscillating magneto and ignition mechanism.*

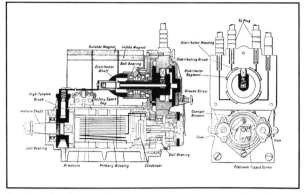

*Sectional view of an armature-type or shuttle-type magneto.*

box-like object mounted to the distributor. As the name implies, the coil contains two coils of wire wound around an iron core. Current from the ignition switch flows through the primary winding on its way to the breaker points in the distributor. The secondary winding, which has many more turns than the primary, acts as a step-up transformer, sending high voltage to the distributor.

## Distributor

The distributor is driven either directly by the camshaft or by gears from the camshaft. In either case, it turns at one-half crankshaft speed. Inside the base of the distributor are the breaker points, the condenser and the spark-advancing mechanism. The cap of the distributor contains the rotor and the high-voltage terminals of the secondary circuit: one for the lead from the coil and one for each of the spark plugs.

## Condenser

This small, cylindrical capacitor is mounted by the breaker points and stores surges of current, reducing arcing between the points.

## Magneto

Most older tractors, and some of the newer ones, use a magneto ignition, rather than what is generally called a "battery system." While many tractors with magnetos have batteries, the batteries are not required for the ignition.

The magneto generates its own electricity and, usually internally, raises the output voltage to the level required for the spark plugs. A separate coil may be found on older tractors.

Basically, the magneto is a permanent magnet generator, coil and distributor all in one unit. Thus,

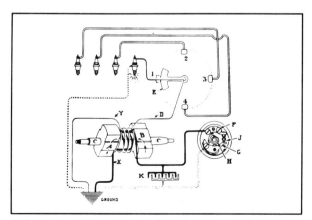

*Induction-type magneto and wiring system for a four-cylinder engine.*

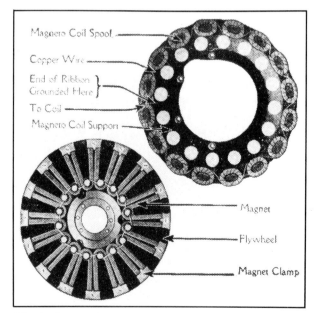

*Flywheel magneto.*

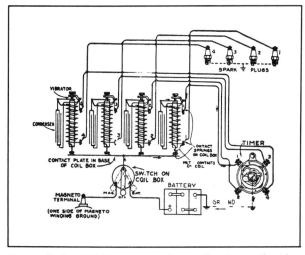

*Four-cylinder ignition system using a vibrating coil with a flywheel magneto.*

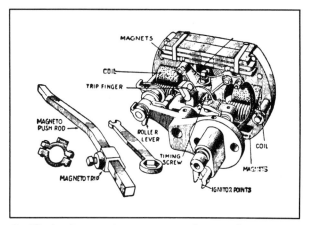

*Oscillating low-tension magneto and integral ignitor.*

the ignition system is self-sufficient and does not require a battery.

To help with starting, most magnetos, except the very earliest, are of the impulse type. This means that when they are rotated slowly (as when hand-cranking the engine), the magneto drive wraps up a spring between it and the magneto rotor about half a revolution; then, the spring is released, snapping the rotor forward and generating a charge of power to fire the spark plugs. This accounts for the clicking noise heard when hand-cranking a magneto-equipped engine.

When properly set up, magneto-equipped engines are very reliable and easy to start. They would probably have been more commonly used on new automotive vehicles today if they weren't so expensive and time-consuming to set up properly.

To stop a magneto-equipped engine, you must ground the magneto to prevent its internal generator from producing electricity. Therefore, a magneto ignition switch is open for operation and closed for shutdown. A common problem in such systems is failure of the switch, or loss of the ground contact, resulting in the inability to stop the engine. In such occasions, it's a good idea to know how to shut off the fuel.

## Battery Ignition Systems

With the ignition switch on and the engine rotating, battery power proceeds through the ignition switch to the primary circuit of the coil, where it magnetizes the iron core, and then proceeds through the breaker points (when closed) to ground. As the engine rotates, the breaker points open, stopping the flow of current through the coil, and the magnetic

field in the iron core collapses. This fluctuation of the field generates the high-voltage current in the secondary windings.

The high voltage goes to the center contact of the distributor and is routed to one of the spark plug leads by the rotor. Being geared to operate at one-half crankshaft speed, the distributor times these operations so that half of the spark plugs are fired each revolution (a one-cylinder engine gets fired every other revolution).

## Diesel Starting Systems

Starting diesels is more difficult than starting gasoline engines. If it's cold, it's hard to generate enough heat by compression to ignite the fuel. Several factors come into play: the temperature of the air; the temperature of the cylinder head, walls and pistons; and the speed at which it is cranked. Because of the high compression of the diesel, it takes about twice as much power to crank it as it does to start an equivalent gasoline engine.

You will probably find four types of diesel starting systems: straight electric, electric with glow

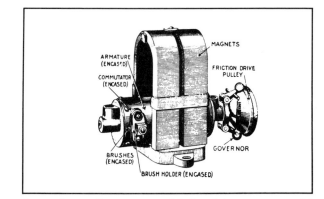

*Low-voltage, direct-current, friction-driven magneto with governor.*

plug, gasoline and gasoline "pony" engine. For details on each, refer to the *I&T Shop Service Manual* for your tractor.

## Straight Electric Starting

The starter and starting system are the same as for a gasoline engine, except more powerful. You will likely find one, or even two, twelve-volt batteries. The starting switch is more robust and will likely be of the solenoid type. In cold weather or whenever the engine is not in top shape, a squirt of ether into the air intake will help a great deal.

## Electric Starting with Glow Plug

This is the same system as the straight electric, except there are spark plug-like glow plugs next to the injectors. When electrical power is applied, they get red hot, much like an electric cigarette lighter. This hot spot becomes the ignition point for the diesel fuel. The circuit is simply a switch on the panel connecting battery power to the glow plug. There is usually a temperature sensor in at least one of the plugs, which closes a panel light circuit when the spot is hot enough.

## Gasoline Starting

International Harvester diesel engines are designed so that they can also be started as carburetor engines. Each cylinder has a third valve, operated by a control rod from the dash, which, when in the gasoline position, opens the passage to an auxiliary combustion chamber. When gasoline is selected, the control rod also closes an air intake valve in the diesel portion of the intake manifold, opens the gasoline passage in the carburetor and ungrounds the magneto, which furnishes current for spark plugs fitted into the auxiliary combustion chamber. You can now start the engine with a conventional starter or a hand crank, as the auxiliary combustion chamber adds enough volume to bring the compression ratio down to about 6.0:1.

After operating on gasoline for about a minute, the control rod is actuated, and the changeover to diesel is made. Everything said elsewhere for the gasoline ignition system also applies to this diesel starting system.

## Gasoline "Pony" Engine Starting

Instead of an electric starter, a small gasoline engine can be used as a starter. The start of the diesel engine is then just like "straight electric," except that sometimes there is a compression-relief device that holds the exhaust valves open until the diesel is up to speed. This is because engines with this type of

starter are often quite large, and the compression relief makes the job of the small engine and clutch easier.

The electrical system of the small gasoline engine is just like that described for gasoline engines.

## Troubleshooting

When you evaluated your tractor before buying it, you were most likely made aware of the condition of the electrical system, if any, right away. One of the first things you should have determined is whether it had a self-starter and whether it would start the engine. Other items beyond that, such as lights and panel instruments, were probably not of high concern.

Once into the restoration, however, there are some ground rules to follow in troubleshooting. First, if something electrical doesn't work, check the connections. Ground connections especially corrode and deteriorate with time and use. Next, check for a blown fuse in the circuit; a fuse is a meltable link, enclosed in a glass tube, that will melt and break the circuit if too much current passes by (indicating the circuit is going to ground without going through the load). There is no fuse in the starter circuit, so if that doesn't work, check something else.

One of the recommended tools is a volt-ohmmeter. Use this to determine how far power is getting into the circuit under evaluation and look for the trouble where it stops.

Make sure that there is power available by testing the voltage of the battery. It is also a good idea to check each battery cell's electrolyte specific gravity to determine the state of charge and to see whether any of the cells have failed. If the battery is good and power is still not getting out, check the terminals. I have had more electrical problems as a result of poor battery connections than from any other source!

The worst part of terminal problems is that low current level will pass, but starter power will not; your lights will work and your volt-ohmmeter will show voltage down the line, but your tractor won't start. For best results, scrape the battery posts until they are shiny and use new, or very good condition, terminals and cables. Some other specific troubleshooting tips follow.

## Starter Troubleshooting

Besides the previously stated problems concerning battery terminals, similar starter problems can be the result of faulty terminals on the solenoid, starter switch or the starter itself. Check for a faulty solenoid, if so equipped, by listening for a click when you turn on the starter switch. Check also for a failed neutral interlock on the shift lever, which prevents the starter from operating unless the transmission is in neutral.

If the starter "whirs," but does not crank the engine, it is likely that the Bendix mechanism is faulty.

If the trouble is in the starter itself, remove it and take it to an automotive machine shop for exchange or rebuilding. You should also replace faulty solenoids and switches.

## Coil Troubleshooting

The quickest way to test your coil's operation is to pull the high-voltage lead, which goes from the coil to the distributor, out of the distributor cap, and place it about ⅛ in. away from the block or head. Then turn the engine over with the starter or crank. You should be able to see and hear the spark jump the gap. Since coils (at least the common cylindrical variety) are inexpensive, replace any that you are not sure of.

## Condenser Troubleshooting

Badly pitted and burned breaker points may be due to a faulty condenser or a poor distributor ground. Some tractors, notably the Ford and the Ford-Ferguson, have a resistor in the circuit to the coil. This is sometimes removed so that the output voltage can be increased to provide a hotter spark for starting. Not having this resistor in the circuit will also cause rapidly burning points. You should replace the condenser every time you replace the points.

## Distributor Cap Troubleshooting

Since the distributor cap handles the high voltage, it is critical to the tractor's operation. Even invisible cracks will allow moisture to enter, grounding out the circuit. Sometimes, burn marks or dirt will make a path to ground, as well. Replace the cap at the slightest hint that it is causing trouble.

## Rotor Troubleshooting

The rotor should fit its notch in the distributor shaft tightly. The copper parts that carry the high-voltage current should not be pitted. The rotor does not actually touch the plug wire contacts, but passes closely enough so that a spark can jump across. Replace the rotor every time you change the points.

## Breaker Points Troubleshooting

These are the switch contacts inside the distributor that are opened by a composite-material cam follower which rides on lobes on the distributor shaft, one lobe for each cylinder. The contacts are closed by a spring, which is an integral part of the breaker point set. Breaker points become worn, pitted and burned with time, and must be replaced.

The breaker points must be correctly adjusted for the manufacturer's recommended dwell (the amount of distributor shaft rotation that the points remain in contact). The manufacturer may also specify a maximum point gap in thousandths of an inch (to be set with a feeler gauge).

When installing new points, set them as close as possible to the specified gap with a feeler gauge, and then check them with a dwell meter while the engine is running. In some cases, dwell can be adjusted from outside the distributor with the engine running. On some engines, it is easier to remove the distributor and do repairs on the bench. On others, making sure the distributor is put back with the same gear mesh is more trouble than it is worth. If the distributor is easily removable, it sometimes works well to take it to a repair shop that has a Sun distributor machine, or equivalent, which will check every phase of distributor operation.

Hard starting is the usual first symptom of burned, pitted or improperly adjusted points. Power will also be off, but this occurs so slowly that you may not notice it. Another likely sign is uneven running at high engine speeds.

## Vacuum Advance Troubleshooting

There may be a device that looks like two miniature pie plates stuck together, face to face, with an accompanying vacuum hose, attached to the side of the distributor. Some tractors use this device and flyweights to retard and advance the time the distributor fires the spark plugs. Some makes rely on the flyweights, or centrifugal, mechanism; you may find some that have a hand lever spark timing control.

## Base Plate Troubleshooting

This is the plate that fits in the bottom of the distributor. The points and condenser are mounted to it. The advance/retard mechanism rotates it back and forth to adjust timing. It should not be loose, and it should have an electrical ground.

## High-Voltage Wires Troubleshooting

Generally, these are high-resistance carbon-core "wires." If bent sharply, the core will crack, and the wire will be useless. Proper functioning of these wires, which go from the coil to the distributor and from the distributor to each spark plug, depends on continuity of the carbon conductor and effective insulation. In the dark, especially in humid condi-

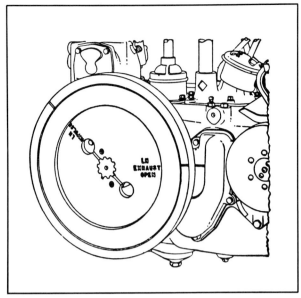

*The valve timing mark on the Model B John Deere flywheel should be aligned with the mark on the cover when the number one cylinder exhaust valve opens.* Intertec

tions, you can see arcing and glowing from these wires, even when they are functioning properly. If you hold one of these wires to see whether the spark will jump to the ground, you are likely to get a good jolt. (It's not the kind of shock that will kill you, unless it scares you to death, because there is almost no current with the voltage; it is more like static electricity.)

Evidence of faulty high-voltage wires will be rough running and hard starting, especially when damp. Sometimes, high-voltage sealant, which comes in a spray, can make a big difference to deteriorating wires and distributor caps.

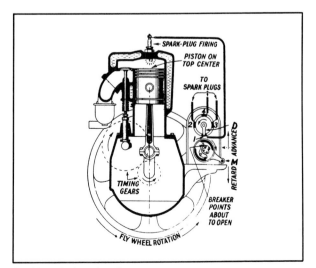

*Ignition timing details.*

## Spark Plugs Troubleshooting

Spark plugs produce the spark that ignites the fuel-air mixture. They, too, depend on insulation, continuity and adjustment to function properly. The need for the ceramic insulator is an indication of how difficult it is to produce a plug that will function under the conditions imposed. That insulator has to seal the high-combustion temperatures and pressures while passing some 20,000 volts through its center.

A good way to tell whether a plug is basically functioning is to remove it from its cylinder, connect it to its wire and then lay it on or against the engine while the engine is turned over. The spark jumping the gap should be visible. Once installed, however, this does not ensure proper plug operation. When compression pressure builds up on it, it is much more difficult for the spark to get across the gap, and it will tend to find an easier path to ground.

The easiest way to check a plug is to replace it with a new one; if the problem goes away, throw out the old plug.

A certain amount of engine diagnosis can be accomplished by looking at the spark plugs after a period of operation. A normal plug will have a gray or light brown deposit on it. Black or sooty deposits indicate too rich a mixture, low compression, weak spark or improper spark plug for the conditions. Oil or oil deposits on the plug indicate leaking valve guides or faulty piston rings.

Spark plugs come in several heat ranges; follow the manufacturer's recommendations to correct plug fouling problems until the real cause of the problem

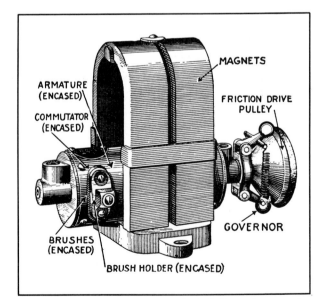

*Revolving armature magneto that delivers low-tension current. It is used in connection with an induction coil, timer and spark plug to form the complete ignition system.*

can be corrected. Also follow the engine manufacturer's recommendations for setting the spark plug gap.

## Ignition System Timing

Proper timing of the ignition system depends primarily on proper assembly of related components, such as the camshaft to the crankshaft gear mesh and the distributor to the camshaft mesh. Next is the fine adjustment of the rotational position of the distributor head. This is accomplished by loosening the mounting bolt for the head, and operating the engine with a timing light connected to the spark plug circuit for the number one cylinder. The timing light is flashed on timing marks either on the flywheel or on the vibration damper pulley in the front of the engine. The timing light acts like a strobe light, so the rotating marks appear to be stationary, and, by moving the distributor head left or right, the marks can be lined up with the indicator per the manufacturer's specification.

Improper timing will result in pre-ignition pinging and kick-back when starting, if too far advanced; or lack of power and hard starting, if too far retarded.

## Magneto Systems Troubleshooting

Magneto repairs can be divided into two categories: minor and major. There are almost no repairs or adjustments that fall into the minor category, and major category repairs require specialized shop equipment. The bottom line is, "If it functions, use it; if it doesn't, remove it and take it in." Proper installation and timing procedures are outlined in the *I&T Shop Service Manual*. Downstream of the magneto, things are the same as for a battery ignition system.

## Conversion to a Twelve-Volt Alternator

There are some good reasons to convert to a twelve-volt alternator from the six-volt generator that your tractor came with. But, of course, none of them

*This Allis-Chalmers B is owned by Joe Polak, Merrill, Wisconsin, one of Wisconsin's largest maple syrup producers. Note the conversion to the twelve-volt alternator.*

apply if you are restoring a show tractor; it must be "original." For the work tractor, however, the alternator will give you two advantages: You should never have any trouble with it, and the additional voltage on the six-volt starter will give you great starting power, even under the most adverse conditions.

Unless you anticipate heavier-than-normal electrical requirements, such as flood-lighting an area with tractor-powered lights, driving an electric winch or some other heavy-wattage equipment, or doing a lot of night work with low engine speeds, there is really not much need for the switch. You should consider the cost-effectiveness.

Often, owners switch to twelve volts to cure problems caused by poor electrical connections, low engine compression or a worn-out starter. When doing a restoration job, however, you should correct these problems. If, when doing a work tractor restoration, you find that your six-volt generator will require expensive repair, you might consider an alternator.

Remember, the alternator has several advantages: no brushes to wear out, full power at idle and double the voltage. To make the change, you will first need a twelve-volt battery, and perhaps, modifications to the battery carrier and hold-down. The coil should be changed, or a resistor installed in the system to keep the output voltage near what the system was designed for. You will probably need a new mounting bracket and possibly a pulley mod-ification to take advantage of the speed capability of the alternator.

Most alternators are capable of 12,000 rpm, and not many old tractors turn more than 2,000 rpm. All the light bulbs will have to be replaced, and resistors will be required to cut the voltage to panel instruments. In most cases, the starter will be OK as is, but check with an authority such as the newsletter people for your tractor.

## Project Tractors

The generator that Palmer Fossum found on the Ford-Ferguson 9N, serial number 357, was of the type found on later tractors. The type used on 1939 models was a two-brush unit with a cut-out regulator. It produced enough electricity to recharge the battery after starting, but was not adequate if headlights were used, so the former owner probably installed the three-brush type sometime during its life.

The smaller, two-brush generators are now quite rare, but Fossum found one in a pail of old parts being offered at a farm auction. He had the rotor turned, and replaced the brushes.

The Farmall A had a jury-rigged, six-volt system, consisting of a car generator and voltage regulator crudely installed. Joe Schloskey also found the battery was shot. Therefore, he decided to convert to a twelve-volt alternator system, since he could do so for about the same cost as refurbishing the six-volt system.

# Chapter 10

# Clutch and Transmission Rebuilding

Because of the close relationship between the tractor's clutch and transmission, the two are covered in the same chapter. Some of the troubleshooting and adjusting can be done together, and such references will be made where appropriate. Nevertheless, each will be described in general separately.

## Clutch Assembly

The term "clutch" really refers to an assembly of parts that temporarily break the connection between the engine and the drivetrain to facilitate

stopping the tractor while the engine is still running. The clutch also enables torque to be unloaded from the drivetrain so that the transmission gears can be shifted. Steam tractors had positive-engagement jaw clutches, but such tractors had engines that could be stopped to engage the clutch. Thus, when the job of driving the flat belt was done and the tractor was to be moved, the engine was stopped and the jaw clutch engaged to drive the wheels.

With the internal-combustion engine, a friction clutch that could be "slipped" to provide a smooth

*A typical clutch plate. The radial grooves are intended to sling oil and other contaminants away from the clutch face.*

*The springs placed around the center hole are intended to prevent clutch chatter.*

*Cutaway drawing of a Farmall Cub showing the driveline from the engine back to the transmission and rear differential.* Intertec

start was appropriate. Many different configurations were tried in the early days. There were externally contracting clutches, internally expanding clutches, cone clutches, twin-disc clutches, multiple-disc clutches and plate clutches.

Although the John Deere two-cylinder tractors, and some others, use twin-disc clutches, plate clutches are now the most common. This assembly consists of a drive plate, a driven plate (also called a clutch plate) and a release mechanism actuated by the clutch pedal or lever. The drive plate is firmly attached to the end of the engine crankshaft at the flywheel. The drive plate seldom requires attention, unless excessive heat warps it or unless it has been scored in service. Then, it may require resurfacing.

The driven plate is a fiber-covered disc with a splined hub that fits the clutch shaft. The fiber, often some form of asbestos, is generally segmented with radially diagonal grooves that are supposed to throw oil and dirt out of the way. Originally, the fiber material was riveted to the disc; later ones are usually bonded.

If, during your test drive, you found the clutch slipping or chattering, the problem is likely a worn clutch plate, although oil leaking on the plates will also cause slipping and chattering. In any case, the cure is to renew the lining and fix any leaks.

The release mechanism consists of a thrust or pressure plate and throw-out bearing. The thrust plate forces the driven plate into the drive plate with a stiff spring or springs. The throw-out bearing, actuated by linkage from the clutch pedal or lever, compresses the springs via the puller yoke, to release the pressure on

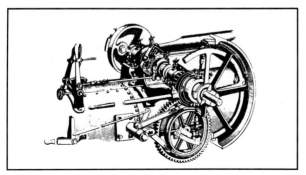

*A friction clutch as used on an early steam traction engine.*

96

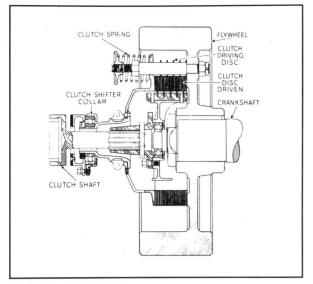

*Multiple dry disc clutch.*

the plates to effect the disconnect. The most likely problem point in the release mechanism is the throwout bearing. Symptoms of trouble are a squealing noise when the clutch is released, rough actuation or no actuation at all.

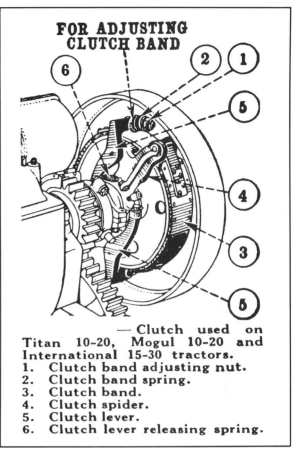

**FOR ADJUSTING CLUTCH BAND**

— Clutch used on Titan 10-20, Mogul 10-20 and International 15-30 tractors.
1. Clutch band adjusting nut.
2. Clutch band spring.
3. Clutch band.
4. Clutch spider.
5. Clutch lever.
6. Clutch lever releasing spring.

*Contracting-band clutch.*

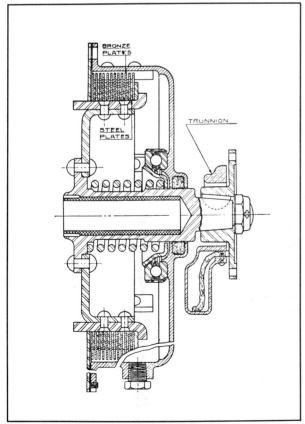

*Multiple-disc clutch running in oil.*

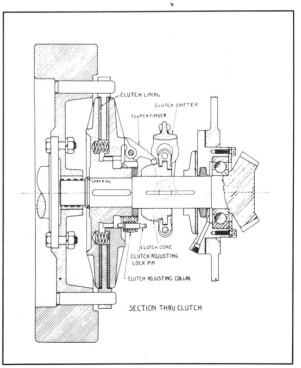

*Twin-disc clutch.*

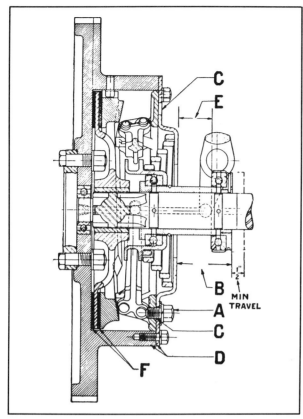

*Plate clutch.*

## Clutch Repair

On most tractors, you can gain access to the clutch by splitting the tractor at the bellhousing. Support one-half rigidly and the other on a wheeled jack or dolly so that it can be rolled away.

It is generally advisable to replace the clutch plate with a remanufactured part. On older tractors, it may be necessary to do the relining yourself. Check the condition of the throw-out bearing, and replace it if there is any discoloration, looseness or roughness. Don't over-grease the parts to facilitate assembly, as the grease may get on the lining.

## Transmission

Transmissions in early tractors were made with cast-iron gears that often were not well-lubricated or protected from the elements so gear wear was a problem. Now, for the restorer, finding replacement gears or getting new gears cast can also be quite a problem. Fortunately, these tractors usually had only two gears: forward and reverse.

With the advent of alloy steels, machine-cut gears with hardened wearing surfaces, began to find use in multiple-ratio tractor gearboxes. These technologies reduced cost, size and weight, and extended the life of a tractor. Most transmissions in tractors of the type the neophyte restorer is likely to encounter are greatly over-engineered (have excess capacity), and do not need to be overhauled. Depending on the severity of service, of course, many farm tractor transmissions are still in good shape after fifty years of use.

## Manual Transmissions

Generally, the type of tractor we are addressing here uses a three- or four-speed manual transmission. If you prefer a newer or larger tractor than the Ford-Ferguson 9N or the Farmall A, you may find a transmission with five or more ratios.

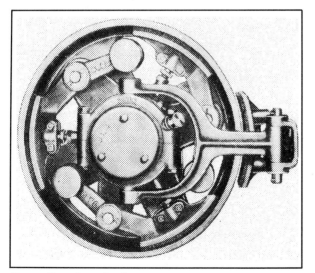

*Expanding-shoe clutch.*

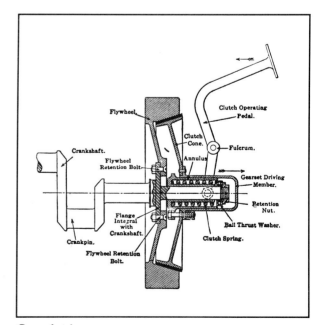

*Cone clutch.*

## Types of mechanical clutches

### Positive

Engagement made by radial teeth

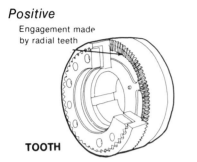

**TOOTH**

Further refinement of the locking-tooth principle. Engagement is between a large number of small gear-like teeth or serrations. Running engagement is possible at up to 300 rpm. Generally available in capacities up to 300 hp per 100 rpm.

**SPIRAL JAW** — Sloping teeth allow smoother engagement

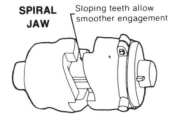

Eliminates some of the objectionable features of square-jaw type. Engaging surfaces are sloped to provide smoother running engagement. Can be engaged at speeds up to about 150 rpm. Available in same sizes and capacity ranges as the square jaw. Runs in one direction only and has a tendency to freewheel.

More complex and more expensive than drum-type but offers a large friction surface and a higher capacity for a given size. The friction surfaces may be flat (disc type) or conical (cone type). Standard clutches are rated up to about 30 hp at 100 rpm. The clutches used in automobiles and most vehicles are specially designed axial-types.

Drive clutch plate is pressed into driven plate

**AXIAL**

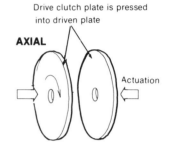

Actuation

### Friction

In expanding type, a set of shoes connected to one shaft expand outward to engage a rim or drum connected to the other shaft. In a contracting type, the shoes are carried by the outer rim and expand inward against a drum. The shoes are actuated mechanically, hydraulically, or pneumatically. The contracting type responds especially fast because centrifugal force helps withdraw the

**SQUARE JAW** — Square teeth lock into recesses in facing plate

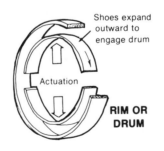

Simplest and most basic clutch. Consists of square teeth which lock into mating recesses in facing member. Provides instant, positive lock-up, but because it cannot slip, cannot be engaged safely if shafts are not stationary or turning at the same speed. Running engagements possible up to about 10 rpm. Available in sizes from 1 to 6 in. in ratings from 1 to 260 hp per 100 rpm.

Shoes expand outward to engage drum

Actuation

**RIM OR DRUM**

shoes rapidly. Thus it is well suited to cyclic operation. Rim or drum-type clutches are easy to repair and maintain compared to most axial types.

Multiple-disc clutches have higher capacity than single-disc types by virtue of stacked alternating drive and driven discs, which increase the working friction surface.

Simplest friction-type axial clutches. Conical pulley sheaves move axially to engage or disengage a belt drive. Suitable for light loads only. An even simpler variation (though not an axial type) uses a standard sheave mounted on a swinging arm to engage or disengage the belt.

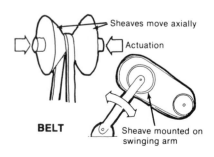

Sheaves move axially

Actuation

**BELT**

Sheave mounted on swinging arm

*Types of mechanical clutches.*

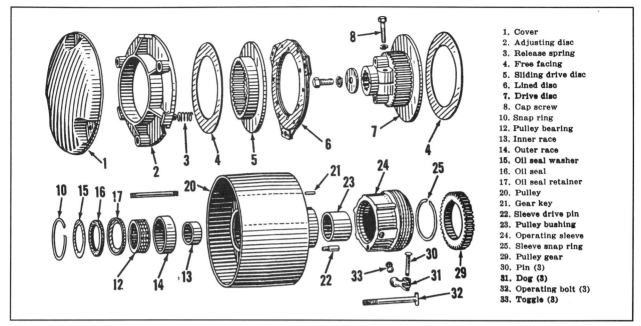

1. Cover
2. Adjusting disc
3. Release spring
4. Free facing
5. Sliding drive disc
6. Lined disc
7. Drive disc
8. Cap screw
10. Snap ring
12. Pulley bearing
13. Inner race
14. Outer race
15. Oil seal washer
16. Oil seal
17. Oil seal retainer
20. Pulley
21. Gear key
22. Sleeve drive pin
23. Pulley bushing
24. Operating sleeve
25. Sleeve snap ring
29. Pulley gear
30. Pin (3)
31. Dog (3)
32. Operating bolt (3)
33. Toggle (3)

*Exploded view of John Deere Model D belt pulley and clutch.* Intertec

*This Ford 851 is being split to remove a failed clutch. Care must be exercised to prevent the engine from rolling over around the axle pivot.*

In cases like the Farmall A, you will find the transmission and differential inside the same housing. Most share lubricating oil with the differential, and the Ford-Ferguson even shares that same oil with the hydraulic system.

Hopefully, you were able to test drive your tractor before you disabled it, and learned about the condition of the transmission. You should have determined that it operated smoothly in all gears, did not jump out of gear under load and was not excessively noisy. Gear whine is not included in the "Inappropriate Noise" category, especially on older tractors, because these gears were often straight-cut without regard for the siren-like sound. The Ford-Ferguson, for example, had straight-cut teeth until 1944; thereafter, it used a helical-cut third gear, at least. For the Ford 8N, introduced in late 1947, all four gears were helical.

## Transmission Troubleshooting

If you couldn't do a test drive, or when you did, things were not to your liking, the first thing you should do back in your shop is remove the top cover. This cover usually contains the shift lever and is secured by cap screws to the transmission housing; make sure that the lever is in the neutral position, remove the bolts and lift the cover straight up. Note the position of the shifting forks as you lift, because you must make sure that the gears are in that same position when you replace the cover and shifting fork.

Once the top is off, you should be able to see what is wrong with the unit. If the oil level is high enough to obscure parts you want to check, you will have to drain the oil. Before you do, know how much oil you will be draining. With a John Deere A, for example, you can expect to drain eight gallons. If the largest container you have holds only five gallons, you will have a mess on your garage floor, unless you can get the plug back in quickly. Check the "Capacities" table in the *I&T Shop Service Manual*.

Many transmissions will have a magnet on the drain plug. Always check for bits and pieces of metal

*The Select-O-Speed power shift control on Palmer Fossum's 1959 Ford Model 981. This planetary transmission provides* *ten forward speeds. Note also the power steering badge, an option becoming popular at that time.*

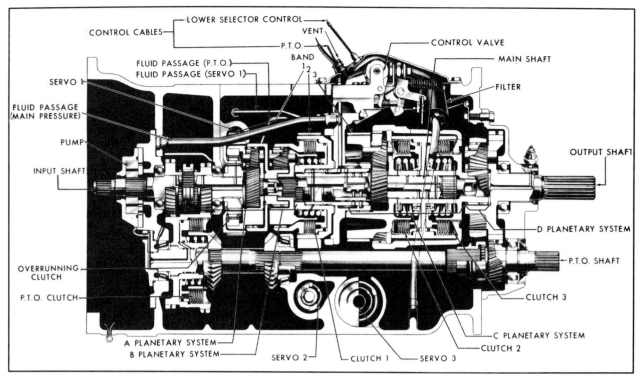

*Cross-section of the Ford Select-O-Speed transmission introduced in 1959. This is a ten-speed planetary power shift unit.*

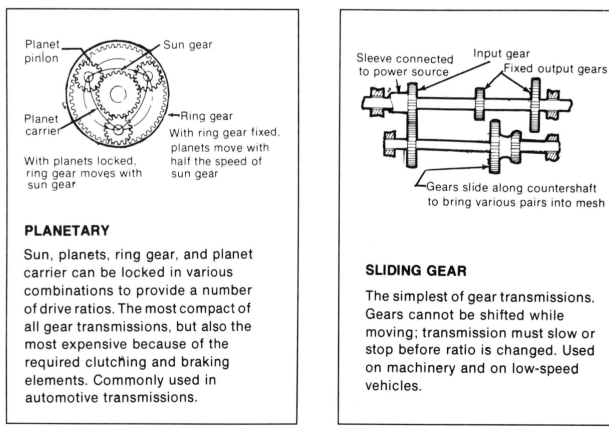

## PLANETARY

Sun, planets, ring gear, and planet carrier can be locked in various combinations to provide a number of drive ratios. The most compact of all gear transmissions, but also the most expensive because of the required clutching and braking elements. Commonly used in automotive transmissions.

*Planetary-type transmission.*

## SLIDING GEAR

The simplest of gear transmissions. Gears cannot be shifted while moving; transmission must slow or stop before ratio is changed. Used on machinery and on low-speed vehicles.

*Sliding-gear transmission.*

clinging to this magnet. If you find more than just wear particles, watch for trouble.

Rotate the gears with your fingers to check for broken or chipped teeth. Also check for radial looseness or roughness in any of the bearings.

Now, if you've found a major problem, you have three choices: fix it yourself, get a transmission expert to fix it or buy a used/rebuilt unit. Deciding to fix it yourself depends on two things: the cost of parts or repairs versus the cost of the used/rebuilt unit, and whether you are up to the technical and mechanical challenge. The 1991 Central Tractor catalog lists several rebuilt four-speed transmissions for $635, plus a trade-in transmission. That is a good indication of the cost and complexity of a first-class overhaul job.

You may need only a gear or bearing, in which case it would probably be better to repair it. Gears and gearshafts run between $25 and $75 each.

You may have to remove more parts than need replacing, just to get at the one you want. Wash all parts removed in kerosene or Stoddard Solvent. It's a good idea to dip parts in clean transmission oil before reassembly, so that they slide together easily and have some lubrication on them to start. If possible, clean the case thoroughly before reassembly, without getting any grit in the remaining bearings.

Pour in fresh oil and then put on the cover, making sure that the forks go back into the same place—and you're back in business.

## Automatic Transmissions

You won't find automatics in tractors earlier than the late fifties, unless you count the friction drives or Model T-type planetaries of the early eras.

Typical of tractor automatics of this period is the Ford ten-speed Select-O-Speed planetary transmission, introduced in 1959. Advertising at the time claimed, "You've enjoyed power steering . . . now enjoy power shifting." This transmission, and others of the time, were just that: power shifts. The definition of a power shift transmission is one that can be shifted from one ratio to the next without interrupting engine power. Automobile automatics are power shifts now, but these early tractors did not have torque convertors and they had up to sixteen forward ratios.

Soon, there were variations on the theme, including torque converters that could be locked in or out without interrupting power. Then torque converters were added to manual transmissions, and shuttle reverses were added to these. With the shuttle reverse, you had a choice of any gear, and the forward-reverse lever determined the direction in

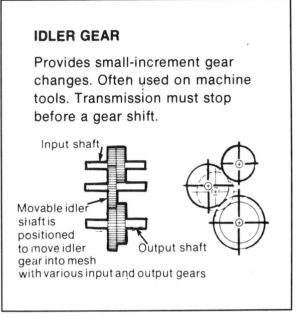

**IDLER GEAR**

Provides small-increment gear changes. Often used on machine tools. Transmission must stop before a gear shift.

Input shaft

Movable idler shaft is positioned to move idler gear into mesh with various input and output gears

Output shaft

*Idle-gear transmission.*

which you would go. The torque converter absorbed the shock of selecting the opposite direction before coming to a complete stop, a great advantage for loader tractors.

A torque converter is a variable-ratio device included in the powertrain between the engine and gearbox. It is a hydrodynamic torque multiplier with two vaned toroids, one driven by the engine and one driving the output and with a stator element in-

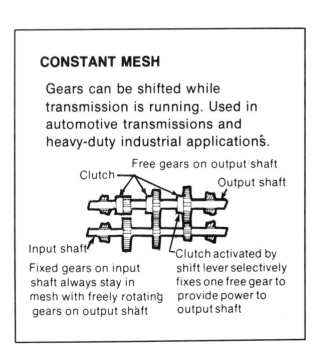

**CONSTANT MESH**

Gears can be shifted while transmission is running. Used in automotive transmissions and heavy-duty industrial applications.

Clutch

Free gears on output shaft

Output shaft

Input shaft

Fixed gears on input shaft always stay in mesh with freely rotating gears on output shaft

Clutch activated by shift lever selectively fixes one free gear to provide power to output shaft

*Constant-mesh transmission.*

## Gear principles

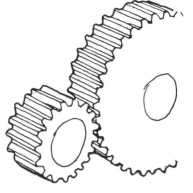

### SPUR

The most common type. Teeth are straight and parallel to shaft axis. Advantages: simple, low-cost, easy to maintain. Drawbacks: have less capacity and are noisier than other types.

### HELICAL

Carry more load than equivalent-size spur gears. Can also be made to operate more smoothly and more quietly. Drawbacks: may be more costly than spur gears; single helical develops end thrust (which increases with helix angle) that requires thrust bearings for gear shaft. Double helix is more costly but avoids end thrust. Herringbone is simllar to double helix but has no space separating the two opposed sets of teeth. It's harder to manufacture to high accuracies. Both herringbone and double helix stand up well for long periods under heavy load.

DOUBLE HELICAL

HELICAL

HERRINGBONE

### HARMONIC DRIVE

Provides high reduction in a small space. Carries high torque. Not suitable for small reduction ratios.

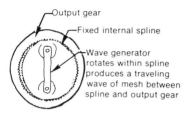

Output gear

Fixed internal spline

Wave generator rotates within spline produces a traveling wave of mesh between spline and output gear

### PLANOCENTRIC

Allows high reduction ratio in a small space. Carries high torque. More expensive than other types. Not suitable for small reduction ratios or for step-up gearing.

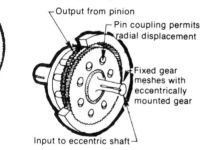

Output from pinion

Pin coupling permits radial displacement

Fixed gear meshes with eccentrically mounted gear

Input to eccentric shaft

*Gear principles.*

## Shaft arrangements

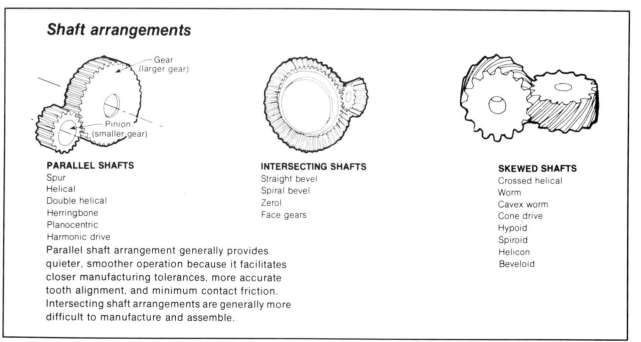

Gear (larger gear)

Pinion (smaller gear)

**PARALLEL SHAFTS**
Spur
Helical
Double helical
Herringbone
Planocentric
Harmonic drive

Parallel shaft arrangement generally provides quieter, smoother operation because it facilitates closer manufacturing tolerances, more accurate tooth alignment, and minimum contact friction. Intersecting shaft arrangements are generally more difficult to manufacture and assemble.

**INTERSECTING SHAFTS**
Straight bevel
Spiral bevel
Zerol
Face gears

**SKEWED SHAFTS**
Crossed helical
Worm
Cavex worm
Cone drive
Hypoid
Spiroid
Helicon
Beveloid

*Gear shaft arrangements.*

between. The stator element is free to rotate with the toroids, but an over-running clutch prevents it from rotating backwards. The driving toroid forces the oil that fills the unit onto the driven toroid with great force. Oil continues through the drive element and is redirected into the driving element by the stator. As the driven toroid accelerates to a speed near that of the driving toroid, torque multiplication (effective gear ratio) diminishes; at stall, some torque converters have the same effect as a 4:1 gear ratio.

Unless there is a lock-up clutch, there is always some slippage between the input and output toroids and, hence, a loss of efficiency. Torque converters are less than ninety percent efficient at best, which means that they generate heat and some sort of coolant is required.

With a torque converter, a conventional clutch is not necessary if the transmission is planetary. If the transmission is manual, a clutch is necessary only to select or change gears.

The planetary transmission's name comes from the way in which planets revolve around the sun. In the common planetary gear set, a sun gear is in the center, three planet gears mesh with the sun gear, and a ring gear circumscribes and meshes with the planets. The planets are held in place by a carrier element. Another name for a planetary gear set is a "differential." The three elements—sun, planets (via the carrier) and ring—can be used as the input or output. All are free to rotate around the center axis, independently of the other two. If torque is applied to one element and another is held from turning, the third rotates at a speed determined by the relative ratio between it and the element receiving the input torque.

Thus, from a single planetary set, there are six possible ratios, plus straight-through (if the planets are prevented from rotating on their own axes). In practical application, however, it is seldom possible to use all options. In the Ford Select-O-Speed, four planetary sets are used to provide ten forward speeds and two reverse speeds.

Ratio changes are effected by means of multiple-disc or externally contracting brake/clutch devices, which stop, or release, elements of the several

*This 1953 Farmall Super M-TA sports a manually operated power-shift torque amplifier auxilliary transmission.*

*Torque amplifier. This is the two-speed planetary unit, used by International Harvester to provide a half-step down in ratio without declutching.*

planetary sets. Neutral can be obtained by releasing an element to rotate that is not connected to the output so that it can rotate.

Shifting clutches, or bands, are sized to stop their related element under full power; thereby, the name "power shift." These transmissions greatly improve the work output of a tractor.

The amateur restorer should not try to repair these. They require specialized repair and adjustment equipment and are often difficult to set up, even with specialized equipment. Setting one up is something akin to adjusting a ten-speed bicycle shifter in the dark.

## Overdrive and Underdrive Units

Much more common in tractors of the type being considered here are overdrive (or road gear) units, which have a separate selector lever to select either direct drive or a step-up ratio. As the name implies, overdrive/underdrive units have two ratios—one higher and one lower than direct drive—plus direct drive.

In most tractors, the engines are mounted forward far from the transmission, and there is usually some space left between the clutch and the transmission. The invention of a gearbox to fit in this space is generally credited to the Sherman brothers. The Shermans were entrepreneurs, importers of Fordson tractors from England, manufacturers of implements and confidants of both Henry Ford and Harry Ferguson. Their first auxiliary transmission was called the Sherman Step-up Shifter, and it was made for the Ford-Ferguson 9N. It handily converts the standard three-speed transmission to six speeds.

It was a small step to add the underdrive ratio. Naturally, the underdrive increases the torque input to the transmission and rear end, but as stated before, these are generally quite over-engineered, anyway.

It should be noted that on most tractors, these units also change the power takeoff speed. Thus, some PTO-driven items operate properly only in direct drive.

The Ford-Ferguson serial number 357 has a Sherman Step-up Shifter, but the Farmall A has only a standard four-speed transmission. Rebuilt overdrive/underdrive units are readily available, at least for Fords, from such places as Tractor Supply, and sell for around $350.

## Torque Amplifiers

Found on larger tractors after the early fifties, a torque amplifier is basically a power shift underdrive unit. There are, of course, several variations on the theme, but the basic function is to provide two ratios for each transmission gear, direct and underdrive, and allow you to get through a tough spot without stopping to shift down and then stopping to shift up again.

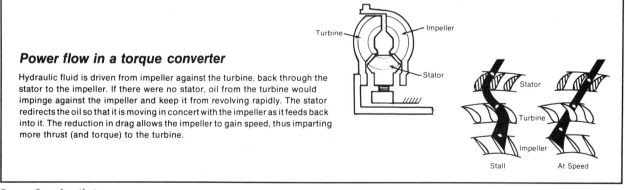

### *Power flow in a torque converter*

Hydraulic fluid is driven from impeller against the turbine, back through the stator to the impeller. If there were no stator, oil from the turbine would impinge against the impeller and keep it from revolving rapidly. The stator redirects the oil so that it is moving in concert with the impeller as it feeds back into it. The reduction in drag allows the impeller to gain speed, thus imparting more thrust (and torque) to the turbine.

*Power flow details in a torque converter.*

# Chapter 11

# Differentials and Final Drives

Between the transmission output and the rear wheels is a planetary differential: gears, shafts, chains and sprockets that comprise the final drive for the tractor. There are as many variations on this theme as there are tractors, but for each, the components generally remain in fairly good condition, unless dirt, lack of lubrication or extremely hard-duty use has caused an untimely demise. If you were able to test drive your tractor and didn't notice growling, grinding or jerking in turns, your differential and final drive are probably in decent shape.

Before getting into the details of these items, a word of caution is in order: Remember, when raising the back wheels of your tractor off the ground, the front wheels do not provide the same kind of roll-resistance as in a car or other vehicle with front springs. A tractor generally has only a pivot for the front-axle attachment. A wide-front tractor front end

*The final drive on the Farmall A includes a gear set that attaches to the axle at the interface shown. It is this gear set that raises the Farmall A, giving it ground clearance suffi-* *cient for a belly-mounted mower deck. The gear set has been removed at this point to replace the grease seal, which has been leaking on the brake band.*

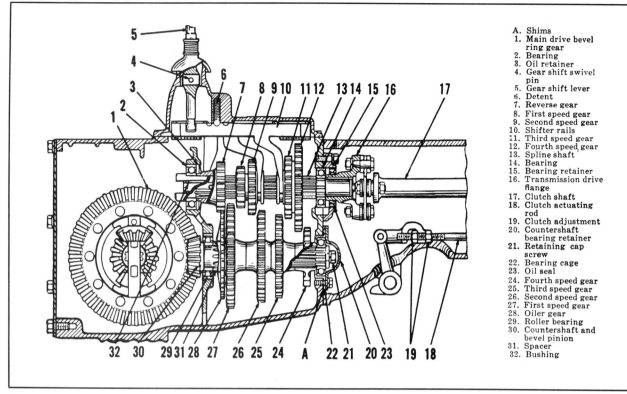

| | |
|---|---|
| A. | Shims |
| 1. | Main drive bevel ring gear |
| 2. | Bearing |
| 3. | Oil retainer |
| 4. | Gear shift swivel pin |
| 5. | Gear shift lever |
| 6. | Detent |
| 7. | Reverse gear |
| 8. | First speed gear |
| 9. | Second speed gear |
| 10. | Shifter rails |
| 11. | Third speed gear |
| 12. | Fourth speed gear |
| 13. | Spline shaft |
| 14. | Bearing |
| 15. | Bearing retainer |
| 16. | Transmission drive flange |
| 17. | Clutch shaft |
| 18. | Clutch actuating rod |
| 19. | Clutch adjustment |
| 20. | Countershaft bearing retainer |
| 21. | Retaining cap screw |
| 22. | Bearing cage |
| 23. | Oil seal |
| 24. | Fourth speed gear |
| 25. | Third speed gear |
| 26. | Second speed gear |
| 27. | First speed gear |
| 28. | Oiler gear |
| 29. | Roller bearing |
| 30. | Countershaft and bevel pinion |
| 31. | Spacer |
| 32. | Bushing |

*Cutaway view of the Farmall A and B Series transmission and differential.* Intertec

*The reassembled Ford-Ferguson rear differential after its rebuild. The unit has been sandblasted and the cast-iron parts have been primed. Everything is now ready for painting.*

provides no more roll-resistance than a single-wheel front end (only a higher roll center), until it reaches its limit of free travel; by then, if you've raised the rear by a single jack, the jack can easily slip out and the tractor will fall.

## Differential

The differential has several functions: It turns the power flow from longitudinal to transverse (except for tractors with transverse engines, such as the two-cylinder John Deere); it provides much, or all, of the final-drive gear reduction (sometimes, a ratio of as much as 7:1); and it divides the power between the two rear wheels.

The direction of the power flow can be changed by using bevel gears. Many drives use spiral bevel, or hypoid pinion gears, which allow some offset from a centerline engagement. Some, such as the Fordson, extend this offset to the extreme and the pinion becomes a worm drive.

The gear reduction taking place in the differential occurs where the pinion and ring gears mesh. On tractors with final drive bull gears or chain drives, the difference in size between the pinion and ring will not be as great as if all reduction takes place in the differential.

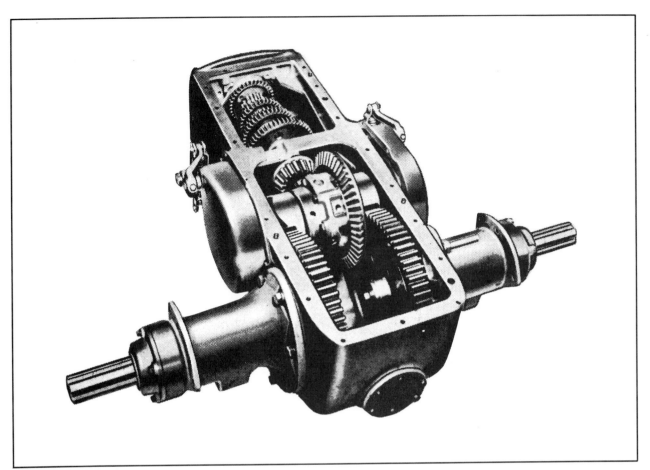

*Farmall H transmission, differential and final drive unit.*
*The brakes are in the drums mounted just ahead of the*
*axles.* Intertec

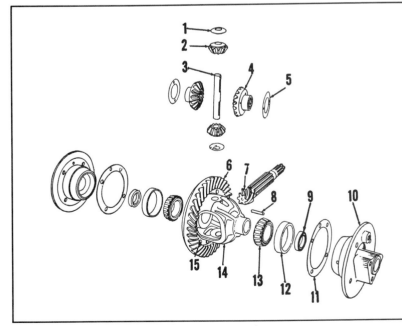

1. **Thrust washer**
2. **Differential pinion**
3. **Pinion shaft**
4. **Side gear**
5. **Thrust washer**
6. **Bevel ring gear**
7. **Bevel pinion & shaft**
8. **Retaining pin**
9. **Oil seal**
10. **Bearing carrier**
11. **Shims**
12. **Bearing cup**
13. **Bearing cone**
14. **Differential case**
15. **Rivet**

*Allis-Chalmers Model G differential showing the compo-*
*nents typical of many tractor final drives.* Intertec

The main function of the differential is to divide the power between the two rear wheels. Differentials are planetary gear sets available in several different configurations, the most common of which is the four-bevel pinion type.

As described in the Transmission chapter, planetary gear sets have three elements: ring gear, sun gear and planet gears held in place by a carrier. In the case of the four-bevel pinion planetary, the ring gear is fixed to the carrier and there are two sun gears, instead of one. With other types of planetary gear sets, each of the three elements can be used as either a power input or a power output. Power applied to one element is divided between the other two. If one of the three elements is held, all power passes from the input to the one remaining.

Thus, in the case of the four-bevel pinion type, if the engine is stopped and the rear wheels are raised from the ground, turning one wheel in the forward direction will cause the opposite rear wheel to turn in the opposite direction. If the engine is operated with one rear wheel raised off the ground, it will rotate at twice the speed, as if both were allowed to turn. If one rear wheel is off the ground and turned (a method sometimes used to start the engine), the engine rotates only half as fast, again as if both wheels were turned.

Differentials are sometimes referred to as "speed-summing gear sets." This means that the rotation applied to one of the three elements comes out the other two elements, divided on the basis of load, or resistance. Therefore, as the tractor is turned sharply, the differential drives each rear wheel so that the torque applied to each is equal, even though speeds are different.

Some early steam-traction engines used straight-gear drives, with over-running drives to accommodate turning. Thus, on turns, only the inside wheel provided any thrust.

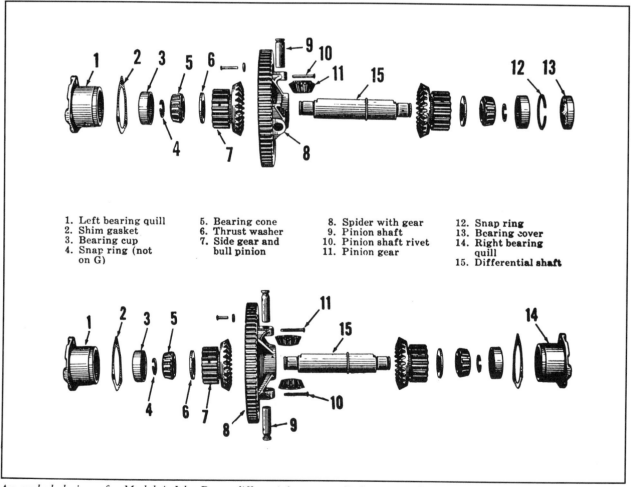

1. Left bearing quill
2. Shim gasket
3. Bearing cup
4. Snap ring (not on G)
5. Bearing cone
6. Thrust washer
7. Side gear and bull pinion
8. Spider with gear
9. Pinion shaft
10. Pinion shaft rivet
11. Pinion gear
12. Snap ring
13. Bearing cover
14. Right bearing quill
15. Differential shaft

*An exploded view of a Model A John Deere differential. Note that, due to the transverse crankshaft of the two-cylinder engine, hypoid, or bevel, gears are not required for input to the differential.*

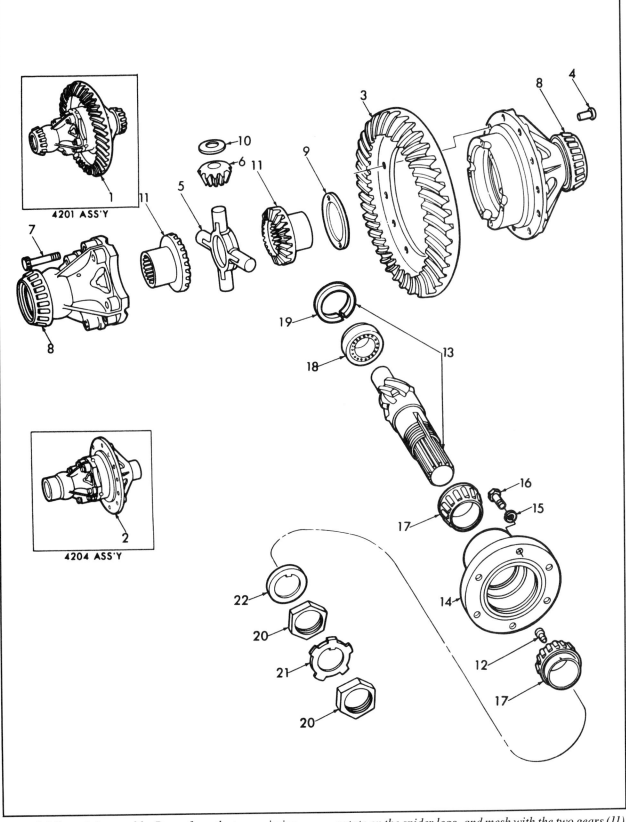

*Typical differential assembly. Power from the transmission comes in gear 13, which meshes with gear 3. Gear 3 mechanically drives the spider (5). Four pinion gears (6) rotate on the spider legs, and mesh with the two gears (11), to which the left and right axle shafts are attached.*

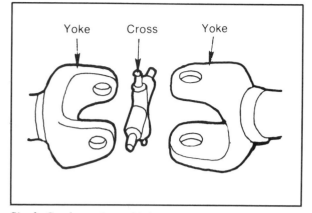

*Single Cardan universal joint.*

## Final Drives

Most of the so-called row-crop tractors have gear meshes running from the differential. Usually, these take the form of large gears in separate housings, concentric with the rear wheels. These mesh with gears on the ends of the two axles, providing gear reduction in the final drive and allowing the axle to be higher for crop clearance. High-crop models often use chain drives in place of this mesh, which allows the axle to be as much as 9 in. higher than the standard version.

Many older designs, such as the John Deere Models D and GP, and the McCormick-Deering Titans and International 8-16s, used chains as the

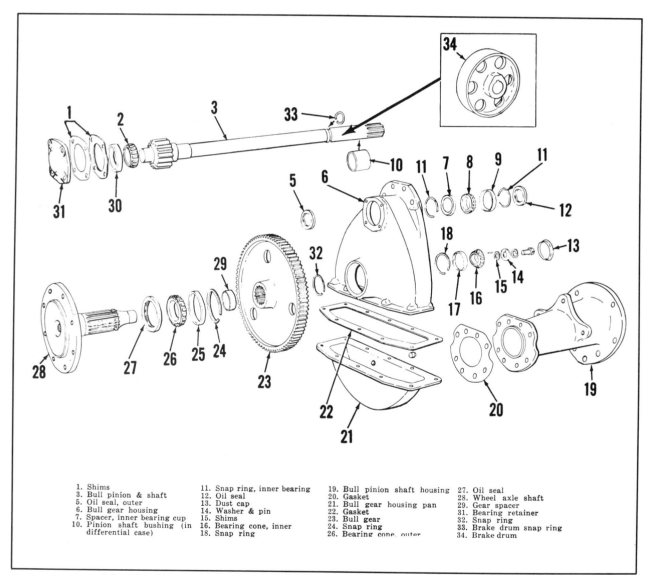

| | | |
|---|---|---|
| 1. Shims | 11. Snap ring, inner bearing | 19. Bull pinion shaft housing |
| 3. Bull pinion & shaft | 12. Oil seal | 20. Gasket |
| 5. Oil seal, outer | 13. Dust cap | 21. Bull gear housing pan |
| 6. Bull gear housing | 14. Washer & pin | 22. Gasket |
| 7. Spacer, inner bearing cup | 15. Shims | 23. Bull gear |
| 10. Pinion shaft bushing (in | 16. Bearing cone, inner | 24. Snap ring |
| differential case) | 18. Snap ring | 26. Bearing cone, outer |
| 27. Oil seal | | |
| 28. Wheel axle shaft | | |
| 29. Gear spacer | | |
| 31. Bearing retainer | | |
| 32. Snap ring | | |
| 33. Brake drum snap ring | | |
| 34. Brake drum | | |

*A cutaway view of the Allis-Chalmers WD final drive and rear axle unit. Note the final drive gearboxes at the ends of the axles, providing much of the overall gear reduction.*

final drive. These large-link roller chains are a nemesis for the restorer as replacements are difficult to find.

## Repair and Adjustment

Adjusting, disassembling and rebuilding a tractor differential are not generally as difficult as they would be for an automobile, mainly because access is easier. Each manufacturer had different approaches and practices, however, so consult the *I&T Shop Service Manual*. In some cases, such as on early John Deere tractors, certain differential components are riveted. Replacing these rivets requires specialized know-how, as well as some new rivets.

There are several methods of adjusting differential gear meshes. Most manufacturers use the shim method, although you will occasionally find adjusting screws. The Ford and Ford-Ferguson tractors have no adjustment for the drive pinion.

Bearings are sometimes shimmed to eliminate end play; in other cases, bearing nuts are tightened until a certain torque (10 to 15 inch-pounds) is required to turn the shaft. Be sure to lock the nut after adjusting.

Rear axle shafts are supported by bearings equipped with oil seals to prevent lubricant from leaking out of the areas in which it is needed. Axle ends are usually slotted and a tapered key keeps the hub from slipping. Shims at the hub usually eliminate end play in the axle shaft. It is a good idea to try to use the same amount of shims on either side to prevent unequal axle extension into the brake; this can cause the backing plate to rub against the brake drum rim; for in-board brakes, this applies to the quill, or stub, shafts.

When working on final drive parts, be sure that you do not allow any oil to drop onto the brake linings; this will cause them to either slip or grab.

## Project Tractors

Neither the Ford-Ferguson 9N nor the Farmall A required any repairs or adjustments to the differential-final drive assemblies. Axle seals did have to be replaced.

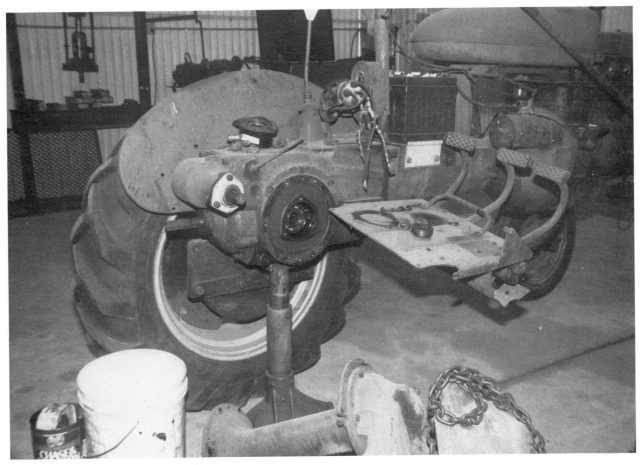

*The Farmall A gets a new grease seal.*

# Chapter 12

# Front Axles and Steering Systems

Nothing differentiates the various brands of tractors more than the front axle and steering philosophy. Some tractors were obviously designed for the narrow front end, even though wide-front versions were offered. Others were strictly wide-front.

One problem that has always plagued the tractor designer was how to get a comfortable steering wheel angle and still have the steering wheel centered in the tractor. The Farmall A is offset to the right, so that the steering rod can go alongside the engine to the steering box at the front axle. The Farmall C, on the other hand, puts the operator in the center, but the

seat and wheel are both higher and the wheel angle is steeper; the steering shaft goes to the steering box behind the engine. The larger Farmalls have the operator on center, but the steering rod goes over the engine; the steering wheel is almost vertical.

Some tractor designers have recognized the desirability of being able to operate the tractor from a standing position: It enables the driver to stretch when confined to the tractor for endless hours, and it provides better visibility. In this regard, there are subtle differences between the Ford-Ferguson 9N-2N and the later Ford 8N. The 8N positions the

*A rare John Deere BR on rubber. Note the radius rods extending from beneath the center of the tractor to each end*
*of the front axle. Any looseness of these rods will cause steering problems.*

steering wheel slightly higher and at a greater angle. That, coupled with a flip-up seat, allows for standing operation.

## Front Axle Systems

Much design philosophy has gone into front-axle configuration. The methods of providing wheel spacing are as numerous as tractor brands. It is interesting to note that the wheel spacing procedure for the Ford-Ferguson 9N-2N tractor is simpler than that of the later Ford 8N and does not require realigning the wheels. When Ford and Ferguson went their separate ways in 1947, Ferguson sued Ford for patent infringement. This, and other slight changes to the 8N, were Ford's attempt to avoid these claims.

One of the more unique front-axle systems is the Roll-O-Matic used on the John Deere Models A, B and G. The Roll-O-Matic is a narrow-front assembly, whereby the two front wheels are geared together in the center, so that they move up and down in opposite directions. The idea is that if one wheel rolls over a rock, the wheel traveling up forces the other wheel down an equal amount and the front of the tractor comes up only one-half the height of the rock, thus improving the ride. In essence, this provides the same results in a narrow-front tractor as in a wide-front. The wide-front axle, with its center pivot, does the same thing, but without resorting to gears.

## Steering Systems

After the brakes, the steering mechanism is the most important feature from a safety standpoint and needs the same degree of attention. Most tractor steering mechanisms are relatively simple, compared to that of a car, and restoration is merely a matter of replacing worn parts and correct adjustment.

The steering boxes come in many varieties, but are generally one of two basic types: worm and nut, and ball screw and nut. Most have some adjustment capability, but occasionally, as with the Farmall A, adjustment isn't possible, and you either have to rebuild the box or find a better one on the used parts market.

Some definitions might help you understand problems you encountered when you test drove your tractor.

## Toe-in

This is the distance by which the wheels are closer together at the front of the axle than in the rear. This is done so that when the slack in all the joints is taken out because the front wheels tend to turn outward in operation, they will not be turned further than straight ahead. Toe-in also causes the outside wheel

to "lead" in a turn, since it has the greatest authority and traction. Improper toe-in will cause tire wear, and the tractor will not continue to move straight ahead when the steering wheel is released.

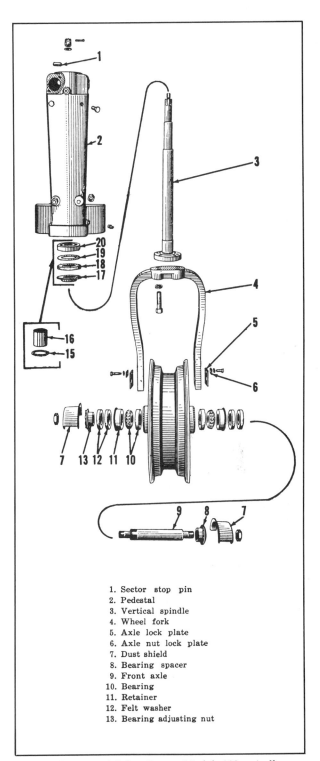

1. Sector stop pin
2. Pedestal
3. Vertical spindle
4. Wheel fork
5. Axle lock plate
6. Axle nut lock plate
7. Dust shield
8. Bearing spacer
9. Front axle
10. Bearing
11. Retainer
12. Felt washer
13. Bearing adjusting nut

*Exploded view of John Deere Model AN spindle-type tricycle front axle.* Intertec

115

## Camber

This is the amount by which the wheels are inclined outward from vertical. The purpose is to put the weight of the tractor over the tire/ground contact spot (the kingpins must point to this spot). This allows the tire to pivot when turned without other forces being induced and makes steering easier. Incorrect camber causes shimmying and jerking of the steering wheel while moving both forward and backward. Perfect camber is not obtained on a two-

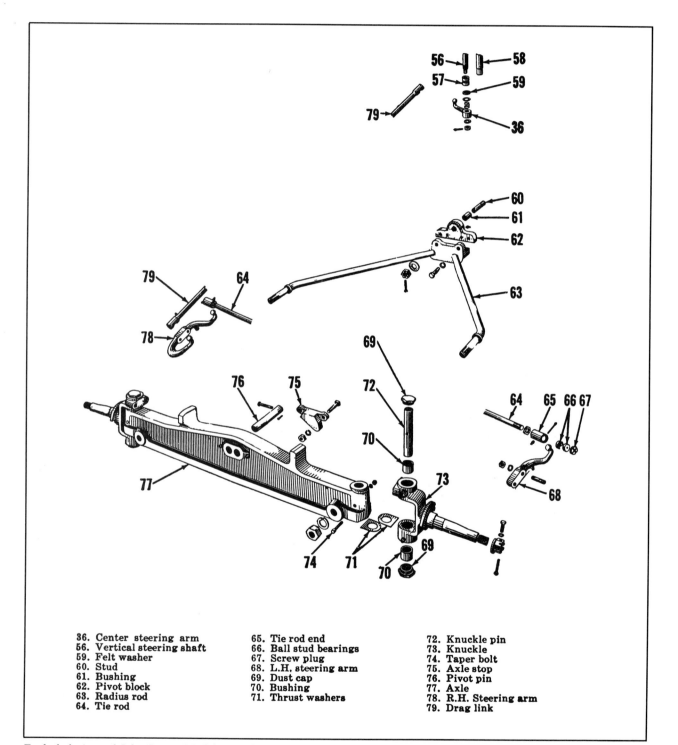

| | | |
|---|---|---|
| 36. Center steering arm | 65. Tie rod end | 72. Knuckle pin |
| 56. Vertical steering shaft | 66. Ball stud bearings | 73. Knuckle |
| 59. Felt washer | 67. Screw plug | 74. Taper bolt |
| 60. Stud | 68. L.H. steering arm | 75. Axle stop |
| 61. Bushing | 69. Dust cap | 76. Pivot pin |
| 62. Pivot block | 70. Bushing | 77. Axle |
| 63. Radius rod | 71. Thrust washers | 78. R.H. Steering arm |
| 64. Tie rod | | 79. Drag link |

*Exploded view of John Deere Model D wide-front axle.*
Intertec

wheel front-end tractor, but the V angle between the wheels is an attempt at achieving it.

## Caster

This is the amount by which the kingpins are tilted back. On a narrow-front tractor, it is the amount the axle is behind the steering pivot. Caster provides steering stability and the tendency for the steering wheel to return to center when released. If the caster is inadequate, the steering wheel will be easily turned to one side or the other, but it will require more effort to bring it straight again.

Too much caster will cause the steering wheel to be pulled from your hand when backing; it will slam into the lock on the side it went to, not a good condition, especially if a steering knob (knuckle buster) is installed.

## Troubleshooting and Restoration

On most tractors, these items are factory-set, except for toe-in. The only way the other dimensions become distorted is through damage or wear. The most frequent problem area on wide-front tractors is worn kingpins. Lift the front of the tractor and grasp the wheel at the top and bottom to see whether there is any free-play. Differentiate between kingpin and front wheel bearing movement; there should not be any from either source.

The next most prominent place for steering difficulties to arise is the linkage joints, or knuckles. These are the tie rod ends, or drag link ends. They are generally replaceable. With the front of the tractor off the ground, grasp the tire at the front and back and try to move it back and forth. Some free-play will be evident, even on a tight system. Locate the source of anything excessive.

When checking the linkage as outlined above, you may determine that the source of looseness is the steering gearbox. If this is the case, check the *I&T Shop Service Manual* to see what adjustments are possible.

*A Waterloo Boy Model N tractor, built by John Deere in 1923, incorporated worm-and-sector gear steering, replacing chain steering as used on earlier Model R tractors.*

On wide-front machines, a common source of steering problems is looseness in the radius rods or other devices, which are supposed to hold the axle rigid (90 degrees to the tractor's center line, while allowing rotation about the pivot). In most cases, rod ends can be shimmed. When checking the radius rods, also check the center pivot; it may need to be rebushed.

When finished, there should be about 1–2 in. of free-play at the steering wheel rim. Steering should be neutral, meaning that the tractor should proceed straight ahead on level ground, with the steering wheel released, and when turned to the left or right and then released, it should smartly return to straight ahead. There should be no hint of shimmy on a hard surface at top road speed, and the tractor should not be difficult to control backing up. When traveling ahead slowly, you should be able to steer full left to full right and back without any noticeable binding or pulling.

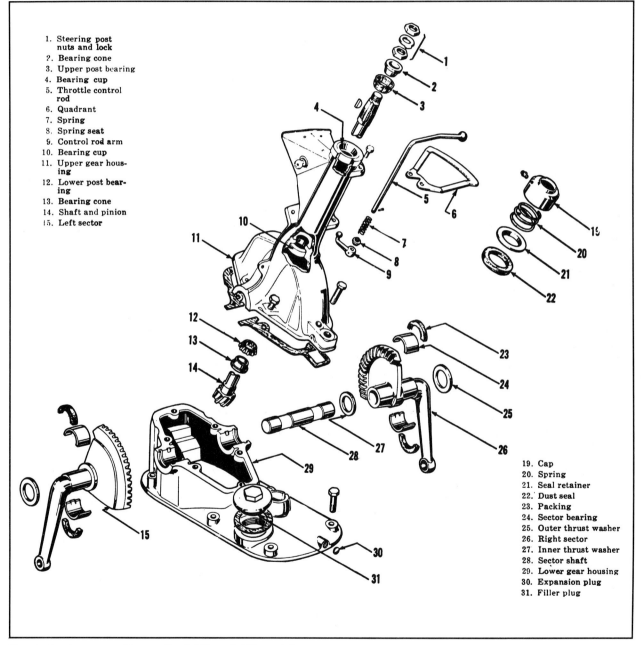

1. Steering post nuts and lock
2. Bearing cone
3. Upper post bearing
4. Bearing cup
5. Throttle control rod
6. Quadrant
7. Spring
8. Spring seat
9. Control rod arm
10. Bearing cup
11. Upper gear housing
12. Lower post bearing
13. Bearing cone
14. Shaft and pinion
15. Left sector

19. Cap
20. Spring
21. Seal retainer
22. Dust seal
23. Packing
24. Sector bearing
25. Outer thrust washer
26. Right sector
27. Inner thrust washer
28. Sector shaft
29. Lower gear housing
30. Expansion plug
31. Filler plug

*Front steering assembly on Ford 9N and 2N models.*
Intertec

## Steering Wheel Rebuilding

There are now companies that specialize in refurbishing both wood and plastic old steering wheels. See the section on Sources for names and addresses.

## Project Tractors

The steering mechanism and front axle of the Ford-Ferguson 9N was found to be in good condition, except for the steering wheel, which was incorrect for that serial number. Palmer Fossum had salvaged a steering wheel from a pre-1948 Ford truck; with the exception of the horn button, this was the same wheel as that used on the first two years of Ford-Ferguson tractors. Fossum had a center button from an early disintegrating tractor wheel, to replace the horn button. It was a simple modification to put the parts together for use on serial number 357.

The Farmall A steering mechanism and axle were sound, except for the steering gearbox, which exhibited a lot of free-play. Since the Farmall A gearbox is not adjustable, Joe Schloskey simply replaced it with a used, but better, unit.

*This 1959 John Deere 530 shows the angled steering column, which was geared to the shaft running above the engine to the steering post in front of the radiator.*

*A nicely restored 1956 John Deere 420. Note the vertical steering wheel position, which was dictated by the requirement for the steering shaft to go over the engine. Following models had a bevel gear set allowing a more comfortable angle.*

The steering wheel of the Farmall A was in quite bad shape, but since this is a work tractor, not a show one, the steering wheel was covered with a commercially available leather wrap.

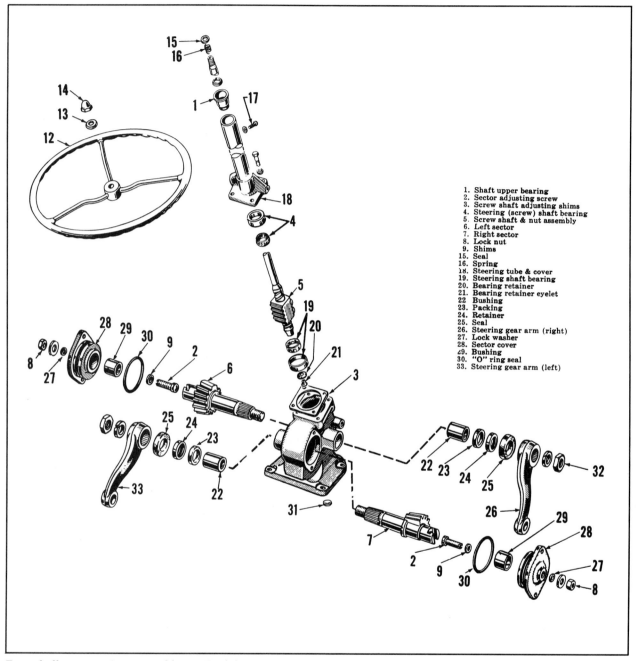

1. Shaft upper bearing
2. Sector adjusting screw
3. Screw shaft adjusting shims
4. Steering (screw) shaft bearing
5. Screw shaft & nut assembly
6. Left sector
7. Right sector
8. Lock nut
9. Shims
15. Seal
16. Spring
18. Steering tube & cover
19. Steering shaft bearing
20. Bearing retainer
21. Bearing retainer eyelet
22. Bushing
23. Packing
24. Retainer
25. Seal
26. Steering gear arm (right)
27. Lock washer
28. Sector cover
29. Bushing
30. "O" ring seal
33. Steering gear arm (left)

*Front ball-nut steering assembly on Ford 8N tractors.*
Intertec

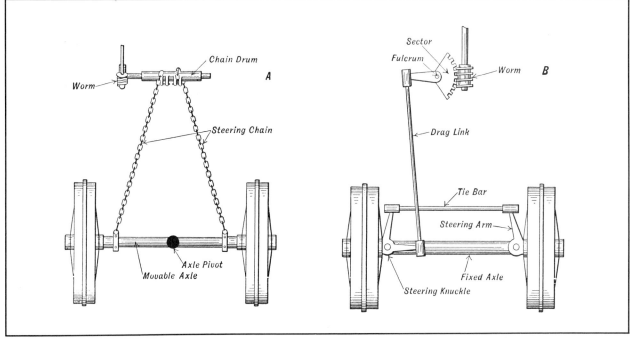

Two fundamental methods of steering tractors. Left, the chain method using tight and loose chains to turn the axle.

Right, the worm and sector gear method with an Ackerman axle.

Some John Deere row-crop tractors, like this 1950 Model A, were equipped with the Roll-O-Matic. This option became available in 1947, and automatically transferred up and down movement equally between both front wheels. Thus, the effect of one wheel going over a 4 in. bump was the same as if both wheels rode over a 2 in. bump.

*Mechanic Tom Marsh begins disassembly of the Farmall
A's steering gearbox.*

*The cast-aluminum dash, steering box and battery carrier,
primed and installed on serial number 357. This unusual
arrangement was used on Ford-Fergusons up through part
of the 1941 model year, when a cast-iron, redesigned part
was introduced. The number visible is apparently a
casting lot number.*

# Chapter 13

# Brake Rebuilding and Restoration

In the old days, farmers didn't pay too much attention to tractor brakes. Indeed, some early tractors did not even have brakes. Car and truck brakes in the twenties and before would be judged totally unacceptable by today's standards, so it is not unusual that brakes on tractors were not afforded much priority.

Early tractors had top speeds of generally below 5 mph, and the rolling resistance offered by lugged steel wheels and the high-ratio gearing offset the necessity for much of a braking system. When the machine was used for belt power through the power takeoff, several large chunks of wood served as a parking brake.

## Brake System Development

With the advent of rubber tires in the thirties, however, tractor speeds began to increase, and better brakes became necessary. Maneuverability could also be greatly improved through the use of individual left and right brakes, especially with the narrow, or tricycle, front end. With rubber tires becoming more and more common, the tractor replaced the horse as the wagon-puller. Now, even trips to town to the grain elevator were made by tractors, often pulling several wagons at speeds of up to 30 mph. Under these circumstances, even good brakes pro-

vide only marginal stopping power, because the two main wheels have only limited traction.

For the restorer, brakes must take high priority. For the working tractor, brakes are required for proper safety and maneuverability. The addition of wheel weights and tire fluid will increase the amount of braking power required for stopping. Brakes are also of utmost importance for the show tractor because they must operate in tight quarters, often with crowds of people close at hand and sometimes pulling or carrying heavy implements. Show tractors are often used to pull a "people wagon" at fairs and thresherees. If you have ten 200 pounders aboard, you've got an extra ton to stop. One of the most severe

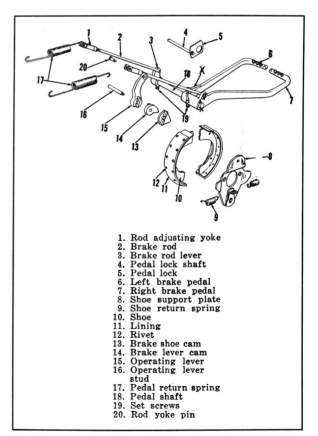

1. Rod adjusting yoke
2. Brake rod
3. Brake rod lever
4. Pedal lock shaft
5. Pedal lock
6. Left brake pedal
7. Right brake pedal
8. Shoe support plate
9. Shoe return spring
10. Shoe
11. Lining
12. Rivet
13. Brake shoe cam
14. Brake lever cam
15. Operating lever
16. Operating lever stud
17. Pedal return spring
18. Pedal shaft
19. Set screws
20. Rod yoke pin

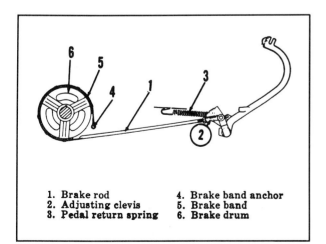

1. Brake rod
2. Adjusting clevis
3. Pedal return spring
4. Brake band anchor
5. Brake band
6. Brake drum

*Typical externally contracting brake assembly, this one for the Farmall A. Intertec*

*Bendix expanding drum brakes, here from an Allis-Chalmers Model G. Intertec*

*Braking power on the left was nil, and as expected, a leaky seal was found. Here, Tom Marsh prepares to remove the seal.*

*The brake and final drive assembly removed from the Farmall A.*

tests of your braking system will come when you load and unload the tractor from a trailer, and you should take extra care when transporting your tractor. Especially when bringing it home for the first time and you are unsure of the brakes, you may want to let it down from the trailer using a chain fall or a come-along cable winch.

## Troubleshooting

Hopefully, you were able to test drive your tractor before you disabled it for rebuilding, and determined its braking power and ability to slide the rear wheels at will, in either direction at maximum speed. If braking power was inadequate, or if the left and right pedals were not even, you would have had to adjust the brakes before continuing. Bent brake actuating rods can account for much softness in the brake pedal and prevent the buildup of much braking power, as can leaking axle seals, which allow grease to come in contact with the lining.

It should also be noted that even at best, most of these systems require a great deal of pedal force. On the Ford-Ferguson, for example, persons of less than average weight or strength will have to stand on the pedals.

During the test drive you would also have noted any unusual noises or operation, such as a failure to release or a tendency to grab or drag when released.

If, while adjusting the brakes, you found binding, corrosion or lack of linearity in the adjustment or couldn't increase the braking power, you would need to further troubleshoot. Unusual noises, failure to release and grabbing or dragging when released are often caused by failed brake return springs—not an unlikely discovery in an old tractor. A tendency to grab, as well as failure to release, are likely caused by paper-thin, or no, remaining lining. Thin lining sometimes folds over when the brakes are applied and wedges the action. The friction of the bare shoes and the remaining rivets against the drum is higher than that of good lining material, which also accounts for brake grab, especially on newer tractors that have the self-energizing feature.

If any of these symptoms are present, or if a test drive was not practical or possible, you should thoroughly overhaul the brake system.

## Brake System Rebuilding

You are likely to encounter one of three types of brake systems on your tractor: externally contracting, internally expanding or disc. Invariably, actuation will be mechanical by means of brake rods, so we need not get into hydraulic brake systems here.

Access to the brake mechanism is different for each make and model, so refer to the *I&T Shop Service Manual* for details. Some vital safety precautions are in order at this point, however. First, brake work will no doubt require that the tractor be raised off the ground. The importance of stable, reliable supports cannot be over-emphasized.

Second, most of the lining material contains asbestos, so avoid inhaling the dust found in the drums. Never use compressed air to clean brake parts

*Mechanic Tom Marsh uses the torch to bake the grease out of the Farmall A's brake band.*

unless they have been washed first in kerosene or solvent.

Third, brake springs are notorious missiles, and you should wear eye protection at all times during the restoration process—especially while rebuilding the brakes. It is also important to use the proper spring tools. A good friend of mine lost an eye to a brake spring.

Newer tractors have brakes and drums much like those found in automobiles, whereas some earlier models have brake units keyed to the inner end of the final drive bull pinion shaft. These often have separate brake compartments with removable covers.

Disc brakes, such as those on some Farmall Cs, Hs and Ms, are also in their own individual housings, splined to the bull pinion shaft. The Farmall units use a ball-ramp type of self-energizer. These, and other types of self-energizing brakes, will have much greater braking power in the forward direction than in reverse.

Internally expanding brakes are more common than disk brakes or band (externally contracting) brakes, but they have a problem not found in the later two: that of bell-mouthing, or coning, the drum. Excessive heat, or just years of strong legs providing the actuating force, may have caused the drum surfaces to distort into a greater diameter at the open end than at the closed end. The local machine shop can often round out this cone by turning the drum on a lathe. In severe cases, it will be best to get a new drum. Bell-mouthing is indicated by uneven lining wear.

Some older tractors, such as the John Deere A and B, require that the brake shaft bushings allow no free play of the shaft. During restoration of an A or B, it is likely that new bushings will be required at each brake relining.

In many older tractors, lubricant leaks into the brake area. Older Fords and Ford-Fergusons, for example, sometimes have an elongated axle hole for the seal to the point where the seal can no longer do its job. Axle housings can be replaced (if better replacements can be found on the used-part market), or the hole can be welded and rebored.

*A stubborn brake adjustment lug gets the heat treatment by Joe Schloskey.*

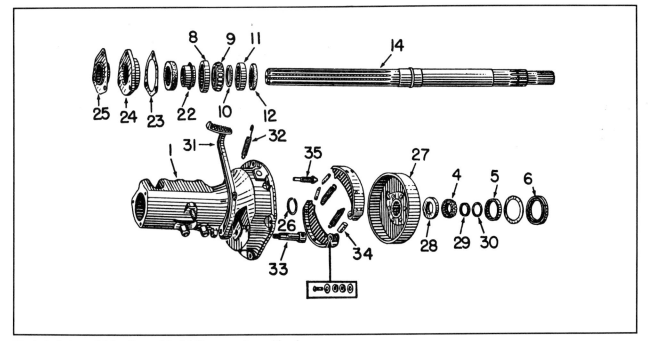

*Exploded view of John Deere Model H rear axle and brake assembly.* Intertec

## Brake Adjustment

In almost all cases, the brakes are adjusted by lifting the rear wheels and tightening the brakes until a slight drag is encountered, then backing off slightly. In some cases, you must remove the "platform" first.

For tractors with left and right brake pedals that can be actuated simultaneously by the right foot, or that can be locked together, it is imperative that the brakes and linkage be adjusted so that the two operate simultaneously. For tractors such as many of the Allis Chalmers models with hand brakes, this is not a requirement. Nor is it required for the John Deere models with hand clutches, or for the Ford-Ferguson models, as the pedals are separated and operated by the left and right feet.

The clutch pedal on the Ford-Ferguson also operates the left brake when fully depressed. Therefore, when adjusting the brake, the clutch must be fully released before braking action begins.

In all cases, there should be about ¾ in. of pedal free play before the pedal begins to cause brake drag. After a brake overhaul, or adjustment, check the brake drum for warmth, an indication that the brakes are too tight.

## Project Tractors

Both the Ford-Ferguson and the Farmall A required brake jobs. The wheels of the Ford-Ferguson were of the wrong type for the year model, so they had to be removed anyway. There was also some indication of oil leakage, so axle seals were replaced.

Likewise, the Farmall A had oil leaks that contaminated the brakes; however, relining was not necessary. The axle seals were replaced and the linings were baked dry of oil by heating them with a torch.

# Chapter 14

# Tires, Rims and Wheels

For several reasons, the tires, rims and wheels on a tractor, especially an antique, are one of the first things to catch the eye. First, the size of the tire causes it to stand out. Next, the wear showing on the tire immediately suggests the condition of the rest of the machine; and finally, a trained eye recognizes whether the tread, the rim and the wheel are appropriate for the tractor.

This is even more true for steel wheels than for rubber. As old tractors wore out their original steel wheels, exact replacements were often not available, and owners had to improvise.

Today, tires, rims and wheels present one of the biggest challenges for the restorer, even for the

relatively common tractors we are following in this book. To do a first-class restoration and not be able to finish it with the right tires, rims, and wheels is anticlimactic.

These thoughts should be in your mind when you are in the process of choosing a tractor for restoration.

**Steel Wheels**

First, decide whether you would be willing to put up with the inconvenience of steel wheels at all. Unless you live in the country, with ample unpaved areas, steel wheels can be prohibitively inconvenient. Some, of course, put flat bands around the cleats and

*An early John Deere BW shows off its round-spoke wheels for conversion to rubber tires from steel wheels. These*  *wheels were aftermarket options, and are correct for the period of this tractor.*

*Wheel weights, such as these on a John Deere 60, greatly enhance traction without the problems associated with cal-* *cium chloride tire fluid. Of course both tire fluid and weights can be used for even better traction.*

*The incorrect sheet-metal rear wheel which came with the Farmall A.*

ribs, and some cover these with the tread sections of old tires. Such solutions more or less solve pavement and mobility problems, but the real purists eschew such compromises. Others leave their steel-wheeled antiques on trailers and unload them only where the going is acceptable. Antique parades through paved areas usually require the tractor be left on the trailer and pulled along the route. Any other movement over pavement, especially asphalt, requires that $2 \times 12$ planks be put down first.

## Rubber Tires

Rubber pneumatic tires will solve the pavement problems, but getting the correct tread for the period of the tractor is not necessarily easy (see the "Sources" section). Also, many of the original wheels have been eaten up by the sodium chloride solution used in the tires for weight, and replaced with later-model wheels that resist such corrosion. Many aftermarket wheels and tires were originally sold. As long as these belong to the time period of the tractor, they are not unacceptable for your show tractor.

For a work tractor, the new-style tread tires are perfectly acceptable, as are almost any kind of rim and wheel that will do the job. For off-set tractors, with the engine not on the centerline, heavyweight rear rims or rim weights are required to prevent tipping.

## Rubber Tire Development

The first recorded incident of rubber tractor tires was in 1871, when a Thompson Rubber Tire Steamer was entered in the California State Fair. This was not a pneumatic-tired tractor, however, but one that used rubber blocks like cleats around both the front and rear wheels.

There was not much interest in rubber tires until around 1928, when Florida citrus growers sought a solution to tree root damage caused by tractor cleats. They modified their steel rear wheels to mount discarded truck tire casings without inner tubes,

*The correct heavyweight cast-iron wheel properly installed on the right rear of the Farmall A, to counteract the weight of the engine being mounted to the right.*

sometimes placing as many as three casings side-by-side on each wheel. The casings were mounted such that the natural strength in the curved rubber was enough to support the tractor without pneumatics. These "tires" provided both flotation and traction and proved so successful that they attracted the attention of the major tire companies.

In 1931, the B. F. Goodrich Company introduced its Zero Pressure tire for tractors, which was based on the same concept as the improvised citrus grower tire. These "rubber arch" tires provided more traction than either solid rubber or early pneumatic tires.

Allis Chalmers engineers began experimenting with low-pressure pneumatic tires and in 1932, fitted an A-C Model U with a pair of $48 \times 12$ Firestone airplane tires on the rear. Later that year, Allis Chalmers announced that rubber tires would be standard equipment for the Model U, using $11.25 \times 24$ tires in the rear and $6.50 \times 16$ tires in the front. The Model U was then equipped with a "road gear," giving it a top speed of around 10 mph. If you ordered your Model U on steel, the road gear was locked out.

Nevertheless, farmers of the early thirties were reluctant to give up their steel wheels and cleats. This was partly due to their poor experience with pneumatic tires on their cars and trucks in the rural America of the time. It was also due to the Depression; most farmers were struggling to hang on to their land and were in no mood to experiment with newfangled ideas.

Accordingly, to dissuade the skepticism, the tire and tractor companies staged plowing and speed contests. Barney Oldfield, renowned race-car driver of the time, was said to have picked up a speeding ticket driving a tractor through a small Indiana town on his way to a race. On September 17, 1933, he drove a stock A-C Model U (except for a special road gear) to a world speed record of 64.28 mph.

---

### Tip: Finding Vintage Tires

Finding the correct style of rubber tires for your show tractor will make a world of difference in the quality of your restoration. Fortunately, along with the growing old tractor interest, a number of vintage tire suppliers offer a wide assortment of tire sizes and types for both front and rear wheels. These include Gempler's, M. E. Miller and Wallace W. Wade; see the Sources appendix for addresses.

---

The same year, a McCormick-Deering tractor on Firestone rubber tires stole the show at a Big Rock, Illinois, plowing contest; and a rubber-tired Allis U pulled a wagonload of farm implements to its destination at a rate of 17.5 mph for five hours official time.

By the 1934 model year, the leading manufacturers were offering rubber-tired tractors, including Allis Chalmers, Case, Deere, Ford, Huber, International Harvester, Massey Harris, Minneapolis Moline and Oliver. Because of the Depression, tractor production was down about eighty percent from the 1930 level, and it wasn't until 1935 that farmers began to re-enter the marketplace in any numbers. Of the wheel-type tractors sold in 1935, fourteen percent were mounted on rubber; that percentage rose to thirty-one in 1936 and ninety-five by 1940.

*Now you know what happens to old, "temporary" spare tires.*

The early years of World War II saw a return to steel wheels, as rubber was a critical war effort material.

## Project Tractors

The Ford Ferguson was found to have the wrong size tires and wheels, and later-type rims on the back.

Palmer Fossum replaced the $6.00 \times 16$ front tires and rims with the correct $4.00 \times 19$ single-rib tires. Fossum found one of these tires at an auction, and one at an antique swap meet.

The rear $10 \times 28$ tires and wheels were replaced with a set of $8 \times 32$ original-equipment tires Fossum obtained from another Ford collector, Floyd Zielke of Nottawa, Michigan.

You may experience some problems when trying to locate new tires of the exact same size number as the originals, as rubber manufacturers changed their marking standards in the 1940s. Where the width number used to be based on tread width, now it is based on the maximum width of the mounted and inflated tire. Thus, if Fossum had desired new tires, he would have had to order $8.3 \times 32$, rather than the original $8 \times 32$.

Fossum had the correct tire valve caps in his collection of old parts, the kind that has the valve core wrench built into the top.

Fossum also obtained from Zielke two of the original 9N wheels, which are now quite valuable, as most have rusted out and been replaced by the newer type. These were installed on serial number 357 with the tires.

The Farmall A work tractor had to have a weighted cast-iron rim installed on the right rear in place of a plain wheel. Otherwise, the wheels and tires were judged to be acceptable as is.

For a work tractor, any tires that will fit are acceptable. Modern 35 deg. bar tires do offer better traction in most instances than the old 45 deg. types. Also, for specialized jobs like lawn mowing, you may want to install a set of low-pressure turf tires.

*Smooth axle hubs had to be located to replace those found on the Ford-Ferguson 9N, serial number 357.*

# Chapter 15

# Hydraulic Systems Restoration

One of the largest step increases in the utility of the tractor came with the introduction of hydraulics. Before then, tractors had two uses: prime mover (power supply via the belt pulley or PTO) and traction engine (for pulling loads via the drawbar). With the introduction of hydraulics, the dimension of lifting and carrying was added, although several makes had employed mechanical lifts prior to the advent of hydraulics.

## Hydraulics Development

The first production tractor with a built-in hydraulic system was the 1930 Allis Chalmers IU with the Trackson crawler conversion. It used high-pressure hydraulics to raise its dozer blade. The 1934 John Deere A was the first wheel tractor to have hydraulics. The Ferguson-Brown, introduced in 1936, incorporated the first hydraulic three-point hitch; it was the forerunner of the Ford-Ferguson 9N. Other manufacturers soon followed, installing various types of hydraulic systems.

With the success of the built-in systems, add-on hydraulic systems soon became available. The idea of the front-end loader was also conceived at about this time. Many designs called for mounting a hydraulic pump in front of the radiator, and driving it via the starting crank passage.

In 1951, Chrysler cars were the first to be equipped with power steering. In 1952, the Behlen Manufacturing Company of Columbus, Nebraska,

*A fine example of a quality parade restoration is this John Deere AN. John Deere pioneered tractor hydraulics on the 1934 Model A.*

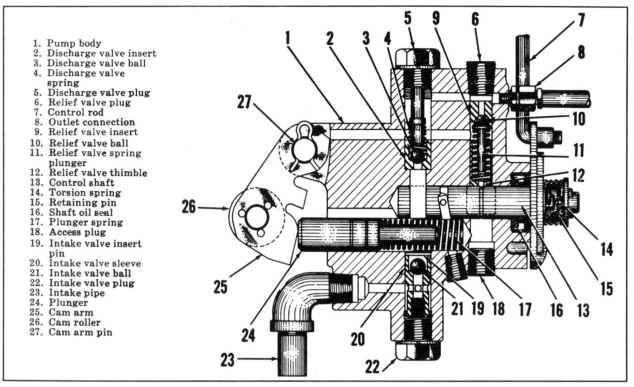

*Hydraulic power lift pump, here of the two-plunger type from an Allis-Chalmers Model B and C.* Intertec

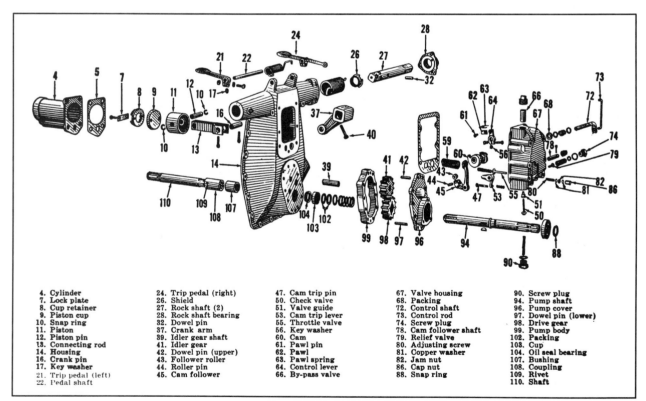

*Exploded view of John Deere Model G power lift. The Model A and B power lifts are similarly constructed.* Intertec

introduced a hydraulic power steering system for tractors, which farmers could install themselves. In most cases, the pump was inserted between the magneto and the magneto drive pad. The trend continued, and in 1956, power steering was made standard equipment on all Ford row-crop tractors.

Power lifting of implements did not originate with tractor hydraulic systems, however. As early as 1886, there was a Peerless steam tractor, manufactured by the Geiser Manufacturing Company in Waynesboro, Pennsylvania, which could be equipped with a steam lift plow.

The 1928 John Deere GP was the first to have an engine-driven mechanical lift.

By 1936, Case tractors also could be equipped with a "motor lift" for lifting and lowering mounted implements. This system used a clutch to connect the engine to a worm drive that actuated the lift mechanism. The tractor driver merely stepped on a starter-type button near his left heal to raise a cultivator, planter or mower. Allis Chalmers, International Harvester, and others, also had mechanical lift systems before World War II.

## Hydraulic Power

Hydraulics is the science that deals with the transmission of energy through flow and pressure of liquids. Components of hydraulic systems include the pump, fluid, fluid reservoir, filters, valves and actuators, or motors.

There are two types of hydraulic power systems: hydrostatic and hydrodynamic. The hydrodynamic variety is applied to devices such as torque converters and powerplant turbines and is not applicable to the uses we are discussing in this chapter. Here we will confine ourselves to only the hydrostatic.

As the name implies, static pressure is involved (as in a hydraulic jack), rather than the mass dynamics of large volumes of fluid flow.

Any liquid can be used to transmit hydrostatic power, but only those based on petroleum oils are commonly used. Other fluids do not exhibit the re-

*The hydraulic lift on this 1949 John Deere MT makes this a valuable little tractor. The MT, with its vertical two-cylinder engine, develops about 14 drawbar hp.*

quired lubricity, viscosity and other factors required by pumps and actuators. For aircraft or other applications where hydraulic fluid fires are a hazard, water- and other chemical-based fluids are available, but specially developed components are required for use in such systems.

"Hydraulic fluid is the life-blood of the hydraulic system. It is pumped by the heart (pump) and provides energy for the muscles (cylinders and motors)," says Melvin Long, noted author and hydraulic expert, in a series on hydraulics published in *Implement and Tractor* magazine. There are several terms applicable to hydraulic fluid.

## Viscosity

This is a property of fluid that resists flow by producing counter-acting forces; in other words, thickness. The viscosity index is an indication of how much the viscosity of a fluid will change with temperature. The higher the viscosity index, the better the fluid will be over a large temperature range.

## Lubricity

This film-forming capacity of a fluid allows it to lubricate the moving parts of pumps, motors and actuators. It is directly related to viscosity: Generally speaking, the higher the viscosity, the higher the lubricity. If the viscosity is too high (say at low temperatures), the fluid does not flow into areas that need lubricating.

To do the job, there must be enough fluid, and it must be in good condition. Too little fluid in the reservoir will result in overheating and aeration of the fluid, and dirt and/or worn out, burned or "varnished" fluids will damage the pump and actuators.

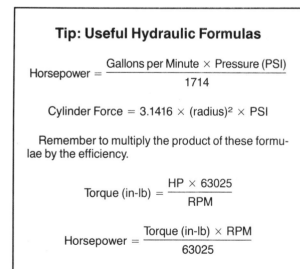

### Tip: Useful Hydraulic Formulas

$$\text{Horsepower} = \frac{\text{Gallons per Minute} \times \text{Pressure (PSI)}}{1714}$$

$$\text{Cylinder Force} = 3.1416 \times (\text{radius})^2 \times \text{PSI}$$

Remember to multiply the product of these formulae by the efficiency.

$$\text{Torque (in-lb)} = \frac{\text{HP} \times 63025}{\text{RPM}}$$

$$\text{Horsepower} = \frac{\text{Torque (in-lb)} \times \text{RPM}}{63025}$$

## Hydraulic Circuits

Just as in electric power, hydraulic systems use circuits. The pressurized flow proceeds to the load via tubing or cored casting passages and then returns to the reservoir, by similar means.

The pump forces the virtually incompressible fluid into the circuit, and the pressure builds up immediately until the load moves or the relief valve relieves. Therefore, system pressure depends on three factors: First, internal leakage limits the pump's ability to raise the pressure further. Second, the pressure in the circuit will not go higher than that required by the load, except when a linear actuator is used, and it bottoms out. Third, the relief valve alleviates built-up pressure.

The amount of fluid delivered to the circuit at pressure determines the amount of hydraulic power. High flow will cause the load to move more rapidly. Flow depends on the displacement of the pump, and how fast it turns. Also involved are several efficiency factors.

Volumetric efficiency is the difference between the displacement of a pump and what it actually produces in fluid output per revolution in normal operation. Internal leakage, or slippage, accounts for most of this loss, but the inability to fill completely and the inability to expel all the fluid taken in also contribute. Volumetric efficiency can vary between seventy and ninety percent.

Mechanical efficiency is the friction that occurs in the pumping mechanism, bearings and seals and causes the power to drive the pump to be higher than the theoretical power required to force the fluid into the system. Mechanical efficiency should be more than ninety percent.

Overall efficiency is the product of the volumetric and mechanical. A volumetric efficiency of ninety percent and a mechanical efficiency of ninety percent result in an overall efficiency of eighty-one percent. Thus, if you have a pump that requires 50 horsepower to turn at its rated speed, you can get only 40.5 horsepower worth of hydraulic power.

## Hydraulic Pumps and Motors

Like the generator in an electrical system, the hydraulic pump produces power and sends it into the system by converting mechanical energy received through its input shaft into hydraulic energy. The energy flows through the system to the actuator(s), where it does useful work.

Hydrostatic system pumps are of the positive-displacement type. This means that pumps can be rated on the basis of their displacement per revolution, or in gallons per minute at their rated speed. A positive-displacement pump will receive and expel the volume of fluid according to its displacement each revolution (less losses due to volumetric efficiency).

Positive-displacement pumps can be either fixed or variable, however. As the name implies, variable-displacement pumps have internal mechanisms for changing the displacement while the pump is operating.

Hydraulic motors are much the same as pumps, except for, perhaps, some changes in the inlet

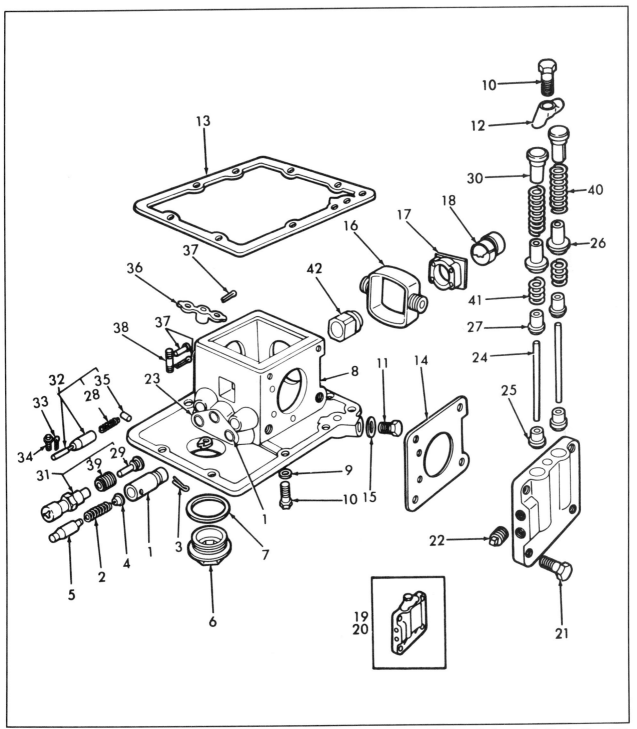

*A Scotch-yoke type hydraulic pump of the type used on the N Series Ford tractors. The yoke, with a piston on each side, is shown as 16. The cylinders are in blocks 19 and 20. The yoke is actuated back and forth by the eccentric (18).*

porting. They receive pressurized fluid and convert it to mechanical shaft power.

There are several types of hydraulic pumps and motors. The first is the gear type, where fluid is trapped in the teeth of two meshing gears. The gears rotate within a close-fitting housing so that the trapped fluid is carried from the inlet side to the output side. The meshing teeth prevent the fluid from being carried all the way around back to the inlet. There are several configurations of gear pumps and motors: two gears side-by-side, two gears one inside the other, and a similar configuration but with a crescent moon-shaped separator. Gear pumps and motors are always fixed-displacement, although there are two-stage, or two-displacement, gear pumps that can shift from high displacement to low, when force, rather than speed, is required.

The vane pump or motor has several (usually five or more) vanes recessed into a rotor which is off-center from the cylindrical housing. As the rotor turns, the blades extend from their respective recesses as they sweep one side of the housing, and then are forced back as they sweep the other. The volume included between two adjacent vanes, the rotor body and the housing progressively reduces as the vanes sweep the fluid (or are swept by the fluid in the case of the motor) from the inlet side to the outlet side.

In the case of the pump, the area under the vane in the rotor slot is sometimes also used for pumping fluid. The hydraulic pressure generated also helps press the vanes against the housing.

Vane pumps and motors can be made to be variable in displacement by including a mechanism to change the amount of offset between the centers of the rotor and the housing. The Ford NAA Jubilee and its near relatives use this type of pump.

The vane pump or motor will be generally superior to a gear pump in pressure capability, efficiency, contaminant toleration and starting torque.

Piston pumps and motors come in a variety of configurations. In general, they are the most efficient, have the greatest pressure capability and last the longest. They are also the most costly and the most common in tractors with hydraulic systems. Most of the varieties of piston pumps or motors can be made variable displacement.

The Scotch-yoke type is found in Ford-Ferguson 9N and 2N tractors and in the Ford 8N. It uses pistons rigidly attached to either side of a square box; a drive-cam oscillates inside the box, driving it back and forth. The back-and-forth motion causes the pistons to operate in their respective cylinders, pumping the

hydraulic fluid. The Scotch-yoke pump works well at fairly low speeds and at medium pressures. It exhibits excellent life characteristics.

In the radial-piston type, the pistons are disposed radially in the cylinder block. Either the block (which rotates) is offset from the stationary center shaft, or the center shaft rotates, driving a cam, causing the pistons to move within the cylinders. This type is not likely to be found in tractors, due to cost, but they are very good from efficiency and starting torque standpoints.

In the axial-piston type, a swashplate actuates the pistons. The swashplate can be stationary, while the block rotates, or it can be the other way around. The pistons, always an odd number, are axially disposed in the block, like bullets in a six-shooter. Axial piston pumps are the best in almost all aspects of efficiency and pressure capability. Many of the later-model tractors will have this type.

The bent-axis pumps or motors are built on the principle of the universal joint, with the pistons axially disposed in one end of the "joint"; that is, the pumping mechanism is at an angle to the input shaft. The whole device rotates but flexes like a bent U-joint: The pistons on the inside of the angle are forced into their cylinders, while those on the outside are pulled out; thus, the pumping action takes place. Bent axis pumps can be made to be variable by including a mechanism to change the angle.

## Hydraulic Pistons

In all of the piston pumps and motors, except for the bent axis and Scotch-yoke types, there can be one of three types of pistons: stick, slipper or ball pistons. As the name implies, stick pistons are merely solid bars of steel, rounded at the actuating end. Slipper pistons are hollow or have a passage from the pumping end to the actuating end, allowing the actuating end to be supported by a hydrostatic film of fluid and preventing metal-to-metal contact. Ball pistons are the same as stick pistons, except they are round, rather than oblong.

A pump or motor with slipper pistons is the best from a life standpoint, providing the fluid is kept in pristine condition. In such devices, other potential wearing surfaces are also separated by hydrostatic-bearing films, so wear is virtually non-existent in normal operation.

## Actuators

Actuators are the muscles of the hydraulic system. They come in two varieties: linear and rotary. The typical three-point hitch system includes one or two linear actuators operating a rocker shaft by means of a bellcrank, or arm link. Typical power steering actuators are of the rotary variety. Hydraulic motors are, in effect, rotary actuators.

The actuator receives fluid from the pump; the relationship between pump output volume and the actuator volume determines the speed at which the actuator output moves. The level of pressure supplied by the pump versus the area of the actuator upon which the pressure acts determines the force the actuator will exert.

Linear actuators are commonly called hydraulic cylinders and are the most common type used in agricultural machinery. Fluid is pumped in one end of the cylinder, driving the piston before it to move the load. Sliding seals are used on the piston and around the piston rod to prevent leakage. These are sometimes called "packings," and can be single- or double-acting. The double-acting ones can be driven in both directions, although the force in the rod-retraction direction is less than the extension direction, because the fluid does not act on the piston area taken up by the piston rod.

In many applications, single-acting cylinders are adequate, with gravity providing the return force. End loaders are a good example of this; one needs only to raise the load with hydraulic force. Even the weight of the empty bucket will be enough to bring the bucket down.

Rotary actuators and motors come in a variety of configurations, including wheel-driving power units. They are becoming more commonplace, although you are not likely to find one in an antique tractor. More and more, they are used to replace PTO drives for trailed implements. Rather than run the PTO drive shaft between the tractor and the implement, just run hydraulic hoses.

### Hydraulic System Safety

A pinhole leak in a high-pressure system can shoot a stream of fluid that will penetrate the skin. Also, remember that fluids are flammable, so beware of leaks coming in contact with the hot engine exhaust. This is especially true of high-pressure leaks that tend to atomize the fluid. Beware of anything that is stronger than you are. Be careful not to pin yourself against something with hydraulic force when you can't reach the valve handle.

### Troubleshooting Hydraulics

The simple test of a hydraulic system is, Does it work? When you evaluated your tractor, you could tell whether the power steering worked and you could determine whether its three-point hitch would lift a heavy implement, such as a plow or grader blade. Beyond those simple tests, though, there is not much you can do for an on-the-spot investigation.

Later, however, especially for a work tractor, when you put the hydraulic components to serious work, a weak system will soon show signs of fatigue. Before you panic, check to be sure that there is enough fluid in the reservoir. Make sure it is not dirty or scorched. Check the filters and magnetic plugs for symptoms. Check hoses for condition and possible kinking. Check the control valve linkage to be sure that the valve is being actuated properly.

If these checks have not revealed the trouble, try to determine whether the problem is with the pump or perhaps a blown actuator packing. You can see if there is adequate pressure by installing a gauge in the system and reading the pressure. If there is no convenient port for the gauge or if you don't have access to a gauge, merely "cracking" a fitting to check for adequate squirting of fluid may suffice. If the pressure is down, or if there appears to be low flow, check the pump drive for slippage or a complete break. If you can get at it without too much trouble, check the relief valve for hang-up or failure. Finally, you may as well look into the pump itself. Fortunately, the parts houses have rebuilt pumps at fairly reasonable prices.

Other symptoms may include a noisy pump, jerky actuator operation caused by air being drawn into the system by the pump or by inadequate bleeding of the cylinders. Overheating is likely caused by inadequate fluid level in the reservoir or by a clogged heat exchanger, if so equipped. It can also be the result of improperly rigged valves, other problems that cause internal leakage or venting of the relief valve.

### Project Tractors

The Farmall A does not have a hydraulic system.

The system on the Ford-Ferguson 9N seemed to be in quite good shape, so nothing was done to it except to clean out the fluid area. Since this tractor uses the same SAE 90 oil for the hydraulics that is used for lubricating the transmission and differential, there was no special reservoir or cooler to be concerned with.

# Chapter 16

# Power Takeoff Rebuilding

Back in the days of the stationary steam engine, the broad flywheel (and flat belt) was the power takeoff. Belt power continued to be a major use, if not the major use, of an engine, even after the traction feature was added. Cross-engine tractors, such as the Case and John Deere, still used the flat belt pulley mounted on the end of the crankshaft. Linear engine machines, such as the Fordson and the McCormicks, used a bevel gear drive to get the belt-pulley out the side in an equivalent manner.

## Power Takeoff Development

It was not until about 1918 that the idea of a rear power takeoff (PTO) for providing power to trailing implements was created. In that year, International Harvester offered a kerosene tractor with a PTO as optional equipment. The McCormick Deering 15-30, introduced in 1922, was the first tractor with a PTO as standard equipment.

Tractor makers continued to include the side-mounted belt pulley as a separate item, but more and more, the rear PTO became common.

Originally, PTOs were connected to the engine's output downstream of the clutch. This meant that whenever the clutch was disengaged, the PTO stopped rotating. This was not a great problem for most implements, but was considered an inconvenience for some. The PTO was connected in this

*The Farmall A normally comes equipped with two power takeoffs: one longitudinal for driving trailing implements, and one transverse for mounting a flat belt pulley. Evidence of leakage caused Joe Schloskey to pull the longitudinal drive to replace the seal. Although leakage was apparently quite limited, he feared lube would be slung onto the mower drive belt and cause slippage.*

manner for two reasons: It allowed the PTO to be engaged and disengaged with the engine running, without having to incorporate a second friction clutch; and it allowed the power to be taken from a more convenient location inside the transmission.

Nevertheless, for equipment such as combines, rotary mowers and the like, it would be convenient to stop the forward motion of the tractor while the PTO continued to turn, so that the implement could clear itself of an overload. With early PTOs, this meant stopping the tractor, putting the transmission in neutral and then re-engaging the clutch. Not only was this inconvenient, but it sometimes allowed the overload to become a clog!

The need for an independent or "live" PTO was recognized. The first tractor thus equipped was the 1946 Oliver. The corporately related Canadian Cockshutt followed. John Deere followed in 1952, with a live PTO for their Models 50, 60 and 70.

To provide the live PTO, a second clutch was added. In some cases, it was operated by a separate hand lever; in others, a two-stage mechanism was used, actuated by the clutch foot pedal. Depressed to the first detent, the main clutch was disengaged;

depressed all the way, the PTO was also disengaged. A gear engagement lever was also provided in all cases to shift the PTO out when it was not being used.

From about 1954, most tractor lines offered live PTOs. Separate belt pulleys also disappeared about that time, and were replaced with a belt-pulley accessory that could be added to the rear PTO. In the 1960s, as the power of tractor engines increased, two standard PTO speeds were established: 540 rpm (the original standard) and 1000 rpm. The use of the higher speed greatly reduced the torque loading of the PTO shaft and universal joints. Some tractors then were equipped with two-speed shifts, so that both speeds could be obtained.

There are two important notes to be made on the subject of PTOs and safety. The first concerns the exposed PTO spline. Many older tractors did not have adequate guards over the exposed PTO spline. This spline was notorious for grabbing the pants legs of the operator as he mounted and dismounted. Even if the spline is guarded or covered by an output shaft, however, any exposed rotating device that you cannot humanly overpower is a peril to life and limb. On this

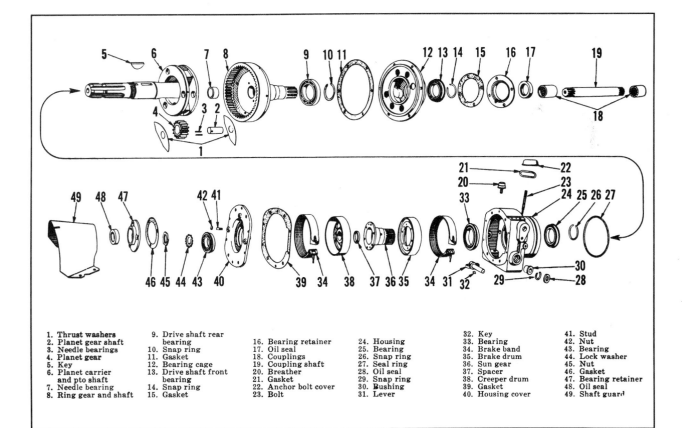

| 1. Thrust washers | 9. Drive shaft rear bearing | 16. Bearing retainer | 24. Housing | 32. Key | 41. Stud |
|---|---|---|---|---|---|
| 2. Planet gear shaft | 10. Snap ring | 17. Oil seal | 25. Bearing | 33. Bearing | 42. Nut |
| 3. Needle bearings | 11. Gasket | 18. Couplings | 26. Snap ring | 34. Brake band | 43. Bearing |
| 4. Planet gear | 12. Bearing cage | 19. Coupling shaft | 27. Seal ring | 35. Brake drum | 44. Lock washer |
| 5. Key | 13. Drive shaft front bearing | 20. Breather | 28. Oil seal | 36. Sun gear | 45. Nut |
| 6. Planet carrier and pto shaft | 14. Snap ring | 21. Gasket | 29. Snap ring | 37. Spacer | 46. Gasket |
| 7. Needle bearing | 15. Gasket | 22. Anchor bolt cover | 30. Bushing | 38. Creeper drum | 47. Bearing retainer |
| 8. Ring gear and shaft | | 23. Bolt | 31. Lever | 39. Gasket | 48. Oil seal |
| | | | | 40. Housing cover | 49. Shaft guard |

*Exploded view of the independent power takeoff unit typical of a Farmall.* Intertec

*With more than 40 PTO hp available, this 1956 John Deere Model 620 is hard to beat for driving a grain auger. For such applications, you can get the horsepower you need much cheaper by refurbishing an older tractor.*

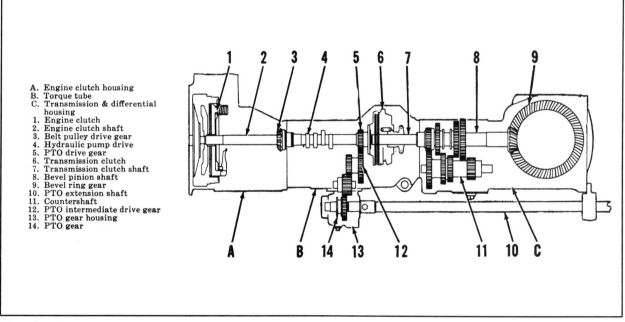

A. Engine clutch housing
B. Torque tube
C. Transmission & differential housing
1. Engine clutch
2. Engine clutch shaft
3. Belt pulley drive gear
4. Hydraulic pump drive
5. PTO drive gear
6. Transmission clutch
7. Transmission clutch shaft
8. Bevel pinion shaft
9. Bevel ring gear
10. PTO extension shaft
11. Countershaft
12. PTO intermediate drive gear
13. PTO gear housing
14. PTO gear

*The Allis-Chalmers Model WD drivetrain, showing the two-clutch method of obtaining a live PTO.*

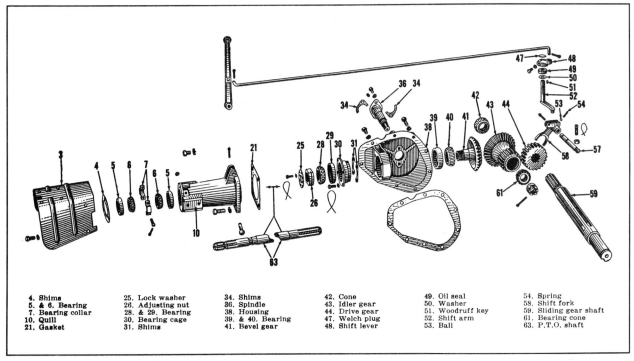

| | | | | | |
|---|---|---|---|---|---|
| 4. Shims | 25. Lock washer | 34. Shims | 42. Cone | 49. Oil seal | 54. Spring |
| 5. & 6. Bearing | 26. Adjusting nut | 36. Spindle | 43. Idler gear | 50. Washer | 58. Shift fork |
| 7. Bearing collar | 28. & 29. Bearing | 38. Housing | 44. Drive gear | 51. Woodruff key | 59. Sliding gear shaft |
| 10. Quill | 30. Bearing cage | 39. & 40. Bearing | 47. Welch plug | 52. Shift arm | 61. Bearing cone |
| 21. Gasket | 31. Shims | 41. Bevel gear | 48. Shift lever | 53. Ball | 63. P.T.O. shaft |

*Exploded view of John Deere Model D power shaft.* Intertec

subject, I feel that I am an authority, having lost my right thumb, and nearly my life, when my mitten got caught in a power takeoff shaft.

The second PTO concern involves the mower blades. When driving a rotary mower, with a non-live PTO, an overrunning clutch attachment must be used. Otherwise, the inertia of the mower blades will continue to drive the transmission and wheels, even though the clutch is depressed—and standing on the brakes has little effect.

## PTO Restoration

There are many configurations of PTOs, but in general, operation and service requirements are similar. For the show tractor, functioning of the PTO is probably not of paramount importance, except for use in driving the dynamometer at engine and threshing shows.

For the work tractor, the PTO is likely to be of paramount importance for driving mowers and tillers and for such farm jobs as driving grain elevators, silo fillers and grain dryer fans.

The most common problem with PTOs is seal leakage. Next is bevel gear problems, followed by clutch problems for live PTOs. Details of each PTO system can be found in the *I&T Shop Service Manual* for your tractor.

## Project Tractors

The PTO on the Ford-Ferguson 9N did not require any repair work. It will be covered by the standard output spline cover with which these tractors were originally equipped.

The Farmall A required a new spline seal, but no other repairs. A V-belt pulley, which came with the mower deck, was installed.

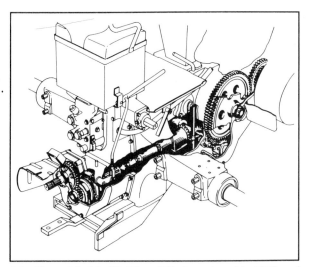

*John Deere Models 50, 60 and 70, introduced in 1952 and 1953, used this type of live PTO, controlled by a separate hand clutch lever.*

143

# Chapter 17

# Body Work and Painting

You are now on the home stretch of your restoration project. This phase requires your utmost care and caution, however, so that the finished product will look as good on the outside as it is on the inside. Here again, restoring a tractor will be easier than restoring an antique automobile. First, unless your tractor fell off a truck going at high speed, there probably isn't any crash damage. Second, there may be rust, but not the type induced by road salt in auto rocker panels and doors. Third, there isn't much sheet metal, trim or upholstery to worry about on a tractor.

## Paint Preparation

You most likely removed the hood, fenders, radiator, gas tank and the like before you started the mechanical restoration, and you also probably pretty well stripped the paint off when degreasing the tractor. Nevertheless, the rest of the paint must come off.

Sandblasting the cast-iron parts is the easiest and most direct route. For the sheet-metal parts, an aircraft metal stripper called Mar-Hyde Tal-Strip II,

made by Talson Corporation of Cincinnati, Ohio, works well. It's strong enough to separate several coats of paint from the metal quickly, with a little help from a blade scraper. There are other good brands, as well. Talk to other restorers or a local body shop.

Exercise due caution when handling, storing and disposing of these chemicals: Wear protective clothing and heavy rubber gloves and use a breathing mask and eye protection.

*Reassembly of Ford-Ferguson serial number 357 begins. After being completely stripped by sandblasting, the cast-iron parts have been given a coat of primer prior to reinstallation of the wheels. The aluminum transmission cover was missed, and will receive a brush priming before continuing.*

*The Farmall A ready for sandblasting.*

Once the paint is removed, wipe the surfaces down with lacquer thinner to remove the residue. You will find that previous repairs will sometimes show up as the paint is removed. Scrape off any body putty and cover the stripped metal with Chem Grip or Metal Prep right away, as rust can set in overnight.

Some final words of caution for the preparation phase: Don't use chemical strippers if there is wood, rubber or plastic in the vicinity, and be careful sandblasting sheet metal, because you can warp or stretch it.

## Sheet Metal Repairs

Most tractor hoods and fenders are full of nicks, cracks, dings and dents. Now is the time to get them smoothed out. Sharp creases may not yield to a hammer and dolly unless you drill a series of $1/16$ in. holes, about 1 in. apart, right down the crease. This allows the holes to take up the metal stretch as it goes back in shape. Afterward, fill the holes with epoxy or lead.

Metal tears may require drilling of the small holes as well, so you can fold the metal back together.

Then, weld a patch behind and finish smoothing with the hammer and dolly. Finally, fill the area with lead or Bondo and grind smooth.

You may need to cut out pieces of metal and weld in new; try to get the seam where it won't be obvious. Much can be done with lead to hide such repairs.

Be careful when applying body lead, as the metal will need to be heated to the point where wiring, rubber and plastic may be damaged. It goes without saying that gasoline or other flammables should not be in the area.

As an alternative, keep in mind that new or used hoods and fenders are available from the parts dealers listed in the Sources section. Also, since you've already got these pieces removed from your tractor, it would be easy to take them to a body shop for repair and painting.

## Paint Priming

Before painting, it's a good idea to remove such things as the steering wheel, battery, tires and engine parts that are not to be the same color as the engine.

*Build up of serial number 357 continues. The proper wheels and tires are now in place. The starter, fan and radiator will not be installed until after final painting of the engine.*

*The biggest impediment to the proper restoration of serial number 357 was locating a cast-aluminum hood as only the first 700 or so 9Ns had such hoods and they are thus very rare. Most, like the one that came with serial number 357, have been broken over the years. Palmer Fossum was able to get this one from another tractor collector.*

The radiator shop has probably already painted the radiator, but other parts, such as the starter, generator and certain belt pulleys should be given a nice coat of black enamel before installation. Get pictures of the tractor type when new to see the details of how it was painted. The *I&T Shop Service Manual,* which contains photos of the tractors obtained from the manufacturers, is one source.

### Primer Types and Uses

Primers are available in nearly as confusing an array as final color paint coats. Primer products include metal etch, primer-surfacers, primer-sealers, and sealers.

### Primer-Surfacers

After you have sanded down the surface to be painted and perhaps used some Bondo to fill in any scratches or dents, the surface will probably still retain some small imperfections such as minute sanding scratches and uneven surfaces. Primer-surfacers are primer products with a high solids content that will cover minor flaws in the surface to be painted.

Primer-surfacers are not body fillers, however. They are not thick enough to fill in bodywork dents and crash scratches; they are only a final finish to fill in slight sanding scratches or minor blemishes.

Primer-surfacers should be sprayed on to the surface in just light coats never more than a couple mils thick and then allowed to dry. When set up, you can wet sand the primer-surfacer for a smooth surface.

### Primer-Sealers and Adhesion Promoters

Primer-sealers and adhesion promoters have the ability to seal one paint layer from another. Sealers are important if you plan on spraying a coat of new paint over an existing paint job. The sealer will protect the new paint from chemically reacting with the old—especially if they are different types of paint.

Enamel paints can be sprayed over an earlier lacquer paint job without a problem, but it is still a good idea to seal the original lacquer coat just in case. Lacquer paints, on the other hand, cannot be safely sprayed on top of enamel unless the enamel is fully cured, something that is difficult to ascertain. When spraying enamel on top of lacquer, then, you should almost always use a sealer to protect your work.

To check whether your old paint job is lacquer or enamel, you can wipe a small dab of lacquer thinner on a hidden section of paint: if the thinner dissolves the old paint, it is lacquer; if not, it is enamel.

In addition to preventing any chemical reaction between two paint layers, sealers are used to ensure good color hold out. Color hold out means that the final coats of paint will not soak into paint layers underneath, causing a dull paint job.

### Epoxy Primers

Epoxy primers have come on the market recently, combining the qualities of metal etch, primer-surfacers and primer-sealers all in one product. These two-part primer products adhere so tenaciously to the metal that corrosion problems are greatly reduced.

Although they can be applied over factory primer, epoxy primers like DP 40 from PPG or EP-2 from House Of Kolor are best applied over bare, clean metal.

### Wax and Grease Removers

Before your surface is ready for a primer, undercoat, or topcoat of color, you should always use a wax and grease remover to cleanse the surface of any traces of dirt, grease, oil, silicone, or other contaminants. Oil from your fingerprints can leave a small amount of residue on a surface that will prevent paint from adhering; silicone or wax from an old wax job will do the same.

## Paint Types and Uses

There are two basic types of paints used on tractors: lacquers and enamels, with urethane paints being a type of enamel. Within each type of paint there are several different specialty paints designed for different uses and types of finishes. The major differences between lacquers and enamels lies in their chemical make-up and how they work on your tractor.

Paint has three main ingredients: pigments, binders, and solvents. The pigment is the base of the paint, providing the color. The binder is a catalyst that promotes adhesion to a surface. The solvent is a liquid that carries the pigment. After the paint has been shot on a surface, the solvents evaporate and the part of the paint coating left is the pigment with the binder as a hardening agent.

Enamels are based on varnish-type binders and dry in a two-step process, thus taking much longer to dry. Lacquers, on the other hand, dry quickly by evaporation of the solvent.

## Nitrocellulose Lacquer

Nitrocellulose lacquer was the wonder paint of the 1930s and 1940s but with the introduction of acrylic lacquer in the late 1950s, it almost instantly went out of style.

There are two reasons why nitrocellulose lacquer went out of fashion. First, the nitrocellulose was a highly toxic additive requiring heavy-duty respiration and skin protection, which was rarely used in those days.

Second, the nitrocellulose lacquer did not contain oils and could not withstand wide ranges in temperature or bumps and knocks—no matter how slight. Therefore the lacquer needed the addition of a plasticizer to keep the coating permanently flexible. The advent of acrylic lacquer solved both of these problems.

## Acrylic Lacquer

Acrylic lacquer adds the liquid plastic binder to the regular lacquer paint, providing a harder, more durable lacquer finish. Acrylic lacquer offers improved ultraviolet radiation protection, meaning the paint will fade slower than regular lacquer if left out in the sun. It also is easy to apply and dries almost instantly.

Acrylic lacquer can be applied nearly anywhere without worrying about having a paint booth to paint in. If you choose one of the new paints that requires additives containing isocyanates, make sure you use proper respiration equipment and work only in a properly ventilated area.

*Anxious to see the finished product, Palmer Fossum temporarily installs radiator, hood, steering wheel and seat.*

On the negative side, acrylic lacquer does not stand up to fuel spills and chemicals as well as the urethane paints. Cracking, often noted as a major flaw of acrylic lacquer, is usually caused by too many layers of paint rather than by the acrylic lacquer itself.

A wide variety of acrylic lacquer colors are readily available.

## Enamel

Enamel is less expensive to use than most of the other paints. It adheres well to most surfaces and requires minimal surface preparation. It does have its problems, however.

Enamel takes a long time to dry and so it must be applied in light coats to prevent running or sagging. The slow drying time also allows dirt, dust and insects ample time to settle.

Enamel is typically a thicker paint than lacquer, and two coats of enamel will give about the same coverage as five to six coats of lacquer. This difference in coverage is something to consider when looking at the amount of time needed in painting and the weight the materials will lift from your billfold.

Enamel can be sprayed over a lacquer finish without a problem, but lacquer cannot be sprayed on top of enamel as it will not adhere.

## Acrylic Enamel

While many individuals continue to use acrylic lacquer to paint their tractors, more and more builders are turning to enamel products. The best known enamel product is probably acrylic enamel, used to paint everything from Ford vans to lawn furniture. Acrylic enamel is less prone to fuel problems when a hardener is used, though it dries more slowly than lacquer and needs color sanding and polishing to create a really great luster.

Acrylic enamel is one of the modern high-tech paints, and is also one of the most durable and weather resistant. The paint is also fixed with chemicals to provide a high-gloss finish. Acrylic enamel has a much quicker drying time than enamel, and once dry, resists scratches better.

Acrylic enamel basically adds liquid plastic acrylic to the regular enamel paint as a binder instead of the standard nitrocellulose. This liquid plastic is naturally harder and more durable than the standard binder. When painting with acrylic enamel, good

---

## Tip: Finding the Correct Color

Finding the correct color for your restored tractor may be the most difficult task for your whole restoration. There are a number of hurdles awaiting you.

First, you will want to find out if the tractor maker or collector club for your brand has records as to paint colors. If so, a premixed paint may be available, in some cases from the original manufacturer if you are lucky. If not, the paint color mix formula may be available and a paint shop can blend your color to suit. Paint chemistry has changed over the years and whether you choose an enamel or a lacquer paint, however, and there may not be an exact matching color available.

If you are restoring a rare tractor, an orphan or simply a model for which no records are available, begin your search by finding a patch of original, unfaded paint somewhere on your tractor. This patch of paint can be invaluable as a source for having a paint shop attempt to match it and then mix paint for you. Good places to look include any shaded section of the tractor that may not have been in sunlight, insides of toolboxes, seats that have been covered with padding and so on.

Second, you need to choose the type of paint you want to use for your restoration. There are pros and cons no matter which type you choose. See the section in this chapter on paint types.

Finally, you may get lucky in finding original records with complete paint codes but then run across problems in cross-referencing old paint numbers with new ones. Paint companies such as DuPont changed the code numbers when there were advances in paint chemicals, such as the advent of acrylic enamels that commonly replaced synthetic enamels. Usually the paint company can provide assistance in cracking the codes; see the Parts Sources appendix for addresses.

The following listing of paint stock numbers covers many of the modern and vintage tractors. With some tractor makers, paint colors have remained the same for years and these new paints will work well. Ask your paint shop or write to the paint maker for color chips.

### Allis-Chalmers
The famous Allis-Chalmers Persian Orange is still available as code 29047 Dulux; PPG Ditzler offers its DAR 60080 to match Persian Orange.

Allis-Chalmers yellow is available from DuPont as 421 Dulux, Imron and Centari as well as 29048 Dulux.

Allis-Chalmers' deep dark green is available from Martin-Senour as code 99-L-11511.

### Case
J. I. Case's famous Flambeau Red is available as DuPont O66DH, NAPA 99L 3727 or PPG Ditzler DAR 71282.

DuPont also offers a Case Power Red as G8156, a Power Orange as 44044 and a Power White as G8157.

Case's early tractors used a dark green provided by NAPA as 99L 8748.

### Caterpillar
The famous mustard Cat Yellow is available from DuPont as H7947 in Dulux, Imron and Centari.

The more modern Highway Yellow is available as DuPont 421.

### Cletrac
Cletrac Orange is available from DuPont as code 017 in Dulux.

### John Deere
John Deere's famous Deere Implement Green is available from DuPont as code 262 in Dulux, Imron and Centari.

Deere Implement Yellow is DuPont code 263 available in Dulux and Centari.

Deere's modern Construction Yellow is DuPont code 43007 in Dulux.

### Ford
Ford's modern dark blue is available from DuPont as 29509.

Ford gray is DuPont code 29665.

### International Harvester
The famous IHC red is available from DuPont as code 7410 in Dulux, Imron and Centari.

### Massey Ferguson
Massey's red is available from DuPont as code 77932 in Dulux, Imron and Centari.

Massey gray is available from DuPont as code 652.

### Minneapolis-Moline
The famous Minneapolis-Moline Prairie Gold is available from DuPont as code 006 in Dulux.

### Oliver
Oliver's green is available from DuPont as code 019 or 030 depending on your tractor's vintage.

### White
White's blue is available from DuPont as code G8164.

dust control is essential; otherwise, the paint will attract dust particles that will settle on the freshly painted finish.

Acrylic enamel is a thick, rich paint and when sprayed on a surface, it provides good coverage, tending to fill in well. A popular myth, however, is that paint fills minor imperfections on the surface. Don't believe it. Any imperfections are actually accentuated by the paint!

Most paint companies now offer a catalyzed enamel. With the addition of a chemical catalyst (sometimes called a hardener) to aid cross linking of the paint molecules, the acrylic enamel becomes more crack resistant, durable and expensive. The catalyst also adds to the gloss and chemical resistance of the enamel finish.

Acrylic enamel also resists ultraviolet radiation and is widely available in a variety of colors.

## Urethane

Many painters are excited about a new family of enamel products known as urethanes. Urethanes offer fast dry times and greater luster combined with low maintenance and super durability. Like very

other great advance, the durability and gloss of the urethanes have a price.

In this case the price is both literal (urethanes cost as much as thirty percent more than a similar lacquer product) and figurative (urethanes are catalyzed with chemicals known as isocyanates). The isocyanates are sufficiently toxic as to require more than just a charcoal filter mask. Most manufacturers require the use of a fresh air mask and complete paint suit with rubber gloves when handling and painting with catalyzed urethane.

Urethane is an enamel by make-up, but not by the way it sprays and adheres. Because of this feature, it is ideal for undercarriages. Urethane is without a doubt the toughest finish, but also the most expensive.

When urethanes were first introduced, color availability was limited. Now, however, virtually any color is available.

## Paint Preparation

For best results, paint the tractor with its wheels off; also paint the wheels while they are removed, and without the tires, if possible. If the tires must

*Finishing touches go on Ford-Ferguson serial number 357.*

remain on the wheels, mask them carefully, as nothing detracts from the finished product like overspray on the rubber.

Dust, grit, hair and other minute particles are the enemies of a quality paint job. Thoroughly clean your "paint booth" before bringing in the tractor. Never paint in a completely closed area. Open a window on one end of your paint area and hang a wet towel over the opening. Then set a slowly moving fan in an opening on the opposite side, blowing out. This should provide fresh air without stirring up dust.

Your air compressor must produce at least 4 scfm (standard cubic feet per minute) at 30 psi. Such compressors are at least 1/2 horsepower. Make sure you have enough air hose to move easily around the tractor. Adjust the nozzle so that it sprays an oval about 3 × 6 in. when a foot from the surface.

For the best source of the right color paint for your tractor, consult the club and newsletter people or a dealer for your brand. Often, a paint manufacturer, such as DuPont, will have the formula for the exact, original paint.

First, you'll need a polyester-based catalyzed primer, such as PPG's (Ditzler) K-200/K-201. Spray on several light coats, sanding in between with #220 grit paper. When you think the surface is smooth, spray a light coat of a different color. Use a sanding block and #400 grit paper. The color difference will now make scratches and surface imperfections obvious. Fill these imperfections, re-prime and sand with #600 grit paper. You're now ready to paint.

## Painting

When choosing preparation, primer and paint use the same brand to ensure compatibility, and eliminate some of the job's uncertainties. Also, follow the manufacturer's recommendations religiously.

Thin coats of paint are to be preferred over a thick coat, as thick paint will chip much easier. Allow ample time for drying between coats. Remember, lacquer dries quickly by releasing solvents into the air, and enamel dries more slowly by evaporation of solvents and by oxidation. Oxygen acts as a catalyst to chemically harden the paint. The drying process

The final touch: tire dressing. Not a requirement for a work tractor, but this one is special. Joe Schloskey jacks up the wheel so he can spin it while holding the sprayer in a fixed position, thereby avoiding overspray. The new Woods mower deck has been installed.

can be accelerated by heat and air circulation, but don't stir up any dust.

## Trim Items

Name and warning decals can be obtained from the parts or decal dealers listed in the Sources section or from tractor dealers. If the directions are followed, applying them is not difficult. The dealer for your brand of tractor or the parts dealers listed in the Sources section can supply you with new or used nameplates, as well. You may also consider having your old plates replated.

Tractors from the twenties used nickel plating, while the thirties saw the advent of chrome-plating.

### Tip: Decals and Painted Insignia

For a parade tractor, the finishing details are of utmost importance. For a work tractor, one need not go to such great lengths, but nice finishing touches will be rewarding. Some of the less-expensive older tractors, such as the Fordson, did not have much in the way of details like pinstriping, but others like the John Deere Waterloo Boy had elaborate scenes painted on the gas tank.

Most tractors will need a set of lettering and logo decals to look finished. Decals, or decalcomania (a French word meaning to copy by tracing), come in two types: water transfer or Mylar. The water transfers are the traditional decals of the type used in model airplane building; they are soaked in water, slipped off the backing paper and applied where desired, then left to dry.

Mylar decals have a peel-off backing and a contact adhesive.

Which kind you use depends on your personal preference, and which kind is available for your tractor. Most decal makers are going to the Mylar type, however, as they are considered easier to apply and give good life.

For a parade tractor, be sure you know which decals to use and exactly where they go. Decal configuration often changed several times during the production run of a particular model. Researching decal location includes looking up old advertising, old photos, contacting the collector organization, and, if it still exists, the manufacturer. Perhaps traces of the original still remain on your tractor. If so, carefully note the size and location before proceeding with paint stripping.

In some cases, a good artist can be persuaded to touch up, or restore, a logo or lettering for which decals cannot be obtained. Also, expert sign painters can be called upon for painting raised letters pressed into the grill, hood or fenders.

Original decals can be found for many makes of tractors; reproductions are also available for virtually every other make. Check the Parts Sources appendix for addresses.

*Palmer Fossum, restorer and owner of Ford-Ferguson serial number 357, applies some final decals.*

For a show tractor, use the type of plating that came with the tractor. For a work tractor, you might consider painting surfaces that originally were plated.

Send the steering wheel to a professional restorer, especially if it's wood or hard rubber. Plastic wheels can be readily repaired by using PC-7 epoxy. Cracks may need to be enlarged with a hack saw for the epoxy to grip. Work the epoxy into the approximate shape and allow it to dry for twenty-four hours. Then, file it to final shape, work it into a glass-like finish with steel wool and paint it with lacquer.

Plastic knobs can also be repaired with PC-7 epoxy. Once back in shape, they can be painted or chrome-plated.

## Project Tractors

The Farmall A did not require much in the way of body work, despite its initial appearance. The sheet metal and the cast iron were sandblasted to bare metal. Some of the more severe nicks and dents were filled, and the metal was primed. Then a nice coat of Farmall Red was applied. A set of decals was obtained and installed. The tractor was rewired before the hood was installed.

The steering wheel was covered with a leather wrapping kit, available from most auto parts stores, and a new seat cover and cushion were installed. The tires were re-installed on the newly painted wheels and given a good coat of black tire dressing—and the little Farmall A looked like brand new. A new Woods mower deck was installed, and it was driven out to the "For Sale" row at the front of the Machinery Hill lot.

The Ford-Ferguson 9N, serial number 357, was not so simple, however. The aluminum hood needed was found in Harrisville, Wisconsin, through an ad in the Ford-Fergie Farmer paper. Todd Harris sold it to Palmer Fossum for $125. One corner was broken off, but Fossum had it re-welded.

The Ford-Ferguson came with rear fenders appropriate to a Ford 8N. By coincidence, Fossum later received an 8N to be restored for its owner, which had fenders appropriate for the 1939 Ford-Ferguson. Fossum checked with the owner of the 8N, and he did want to trade for the right fenders for his tractor—thus serial number 357 got a pair of the right fenders.

Fossum traded a pair of original-equipment rear rims that he had for an aluminum dash panel to replace a steel one he found on serial number 357. The panel was cracked and required re-welding.

As previously mentioned, the steering wheel came from a 1946 Ford truck. He removed the horn

*Ready for another fifty years of work, this restored John Deere GP is being watched over by a horse, who seems none too happy about it.*

button and installed a center cover from a seriously deteriorated 1939 tractor wheel. The result is the correct, four-spoke wheel, just like serial number 357 had originally.

The cast-aluminum grille is new, and cost Fossum $175. It's a replica, cast by Rosewood Foundry and Machinery of Rosewood, Ohio. The foundry is run by Duane Hillman, a tractor restoration expert in his own right.

The aluminum hood was stripped to bare metal for painting, using a chemical stripper. The rear fenders were sandblasted bare, as was the cast iron, wheels and the rest.

Ford-Ferguson gray paint, Martin Senour number 60-19, was obtained from the local NAPA dealer in Northfield, Minnesota. This was applied using some hardener to increase the shine.

The hood emblems used on 1939 and 1940 Ford-Fergusons had chrome-plated raised letters; serial number 357 did not have this kind when Fossum got it. He got the correct Ford emblem in a box of parts at a swap meet and the Ferguson System emblem off of a broken aluminum grille that came with another 9N. He obtained a seat cover and cushion of the type supplied to dealers from the manufacturer and installed it as the final touch.

Serial number 357 now looks as much like it did when it rolled off the assembly line as Palmer Fossum could make it—with the exception of the fancy seat cushion. Close examination of the paint job will reveal slightly more gloss and reflection than the original had. The Ford-Ferguson 9N looks like it's ready for another fifty years of service. Henry and Harry would be proud.

*The instrument panel of this classic John Deere 830 includes a tachometer, ammeter, fuel gauge, oil-pressure gauge and coolant temperature gauge.*

## Tip: Panel Gauge Restoration

One of the most troublesome details on an old tractor is that of panel instruments. It's one thing to make them work; another to make them look good.

The first and easiest step in checking to see if a mechanical gauge is broken is to make certain the drive cable is working. Clean the cable and housing out with a spray electrical cleaner and then lube the cable before replacing it in the housing.

For electric gauges, the first and easiest step is to make certain all contacts are good and that the wires have not shorted out at any point along their length.

If the gauge itself is broken, you may be better off replacing it. Reproduction gauges are often advertized in collector magazines. Also Stewart-Warner made a lot of the gauges for the old tractors, and they still make some that are much the same. Always check the local auto parts store before you panic.

Cosmetic restoration of a working gauge is easier. Chrome bezels around the edges of the gauges can be cleaned with a metal polish or a chrome cleaner. Lenses can be polished with a plastic polish and then washed clean with a window cleaner.

You can often touch up the face of the gauge with an indelible Magic Marker or look for a replacement gauge face.

The needle can be touched up to look just like new by using a Magic Marker as well. Never use paint on the needle as the paint weighs more than you would think; it can set the needle off balance and slow down its operation, perhaps even jamming the gauge over time.

There are a number of professional gauge restorers who can do the job for you or step in when you get over your head. Check the Parts Sources appendix for addresses.

# Chapter 18

# Project Tractors: Ford 9N and Farmall A

At this writing, the work on the two project tractors is finished; in fact, the Farmall A work tractor has been sold and is doing the mowing for Steve Williams, owner of Satellite Die Casting of Ladysmith, Wisconsin. Palmer Fossum's Ford-Ferguson 9N parade tractor has appeared in its first parade, at the Stephenson County (Illinois) Antique Engine Club Steam Threshing Antique Display.

Joe Schloskey sold the Farmall A for $2,950 with the new Woods mower deck installed. Therefore the "value" of it is well established. The value of the Ford-Ferguson is not so readily established, as Palmer Fossum is not anxious to sell it at this time. Nevertheless, three experienced Ford collectors were polled as to its value, and two sales of somewhat similar tractors were investigated, which leads us to conclude that such a tractor as serial number 357

should bring $7,000 to $9,000. The high-end number might get Palmer to change his mind on keeping the tractor, since he also has serial number 364 Ford-Ferguson in equally nice shape.

The cost of restoring the two project tractors will now be presented to the best of our abilities. Bear in mind, however, that one of the biggest variables is what is called "the luck of the scrounge." Both Joe Schloskey and Palmer Fossum are somewhat better off than most in this regard, because each has an extensive backyard "parts department." It's difficult, for example, to put a value on the steering box for the Farmall A which Joe got off a tractor on the back lot, but we'll try—using some used parts catalogs and best guesses. Also, since both Joe and Palmer are in the parts business, they can get much of what they need at wholesale prices.

The following table lists the major categories, and gives the estimated value of parts and labor to do the work mentioned in the various chapters.

*Roll-out! The little Farmall A looks much the same as it did in 1939, except for the 12 volt alternator, of course.*

*Joe, and Joe's father, Lyle Schloskey, who ran Machinery Hill until Joe took over, pose with the finished Farmall A.*

| Components | Farmall A | Ford-Ferguson |
|---|---|---|
| Brakes | $ 50 | $ 110 |
| Carburetor | 25 | 40 |
| Clutch and Transmission | 0 | 115 |
| Cooling System | 45 | 40 |
| Differential and Final Drive | 25 | 360 |
| Engine | 500 | 750 |
| Front Axle and Steering | 185 | 120 |
| Governor | 45 | 75 |
| Hydraulic System | 0 | 0 |
| Ignition and Electrical System | 200 | 150 |
| Power Takeoff | 35 | 10 |
| Tires, Rims and Wheels | 35 | 350 |
| Trim, Paint and Cosmetics | 200 | 1,200 |
| Subtotal | $1,345 | $3,320 |
| Price Initially Paid for Tractor | 500 | 850 |
| Total | $1,845 | $4,170 |

Selling the Farmall A for $2950 means Joe made a small profit on the tractor, itself, and normal profit on the mower deck. As we said in the beginning, Joe's main business is the refurbishment and sale of heavy logging and construction equipment, as well as being

*Lyle Schloskey mows a round with the newly restored Farmall A.*

*Proof of the pudding. Joe Schloskey makes the first cutting with the Farmall A and the new Woods mower deck.*

*Roll out of the parade tractor, Ford-Ferguson serial number 357.*

*Palmer Fossum sits proudly astride his finished work. Serial number 357 was probably built during the first week of Ford-Ferguson tractor production back in 1939.*

*The classic Art Deco lines of the Ford-Ferguson 9N are revealed as serial number 357 sits along Palmer Fossum's driveway in Northfield, Minnesota. Note the smooth rear axle hubs and the early type aluminum grille. Serial number 357 also has an aluminum hood, steering pedestal, instrument panel, transmission cover and battery carrier. Cast aluminum was widely used on the earliest 9Ns as steel stamping equipment was not ready in time for the start of production. The fragility of cast aluminum means that these parts have largely been broken and replaced with steel over the years. Thus, correct restoration of serial number 357 with all these original parts is quite an accomplishment.*

a dealer for Woods mowers. Since rejuvenating a tractor such as the Farmall A is done in slack time, it is probably proper from an accounting standpoint, not to expect to fully recover overhead costs and normal profit.

The difference in the cost of restoring serial number 357 Ford-Ferguson and its estimated value comes from its rareness, and from the fact that all the correspondingly rare parts have been found and added to it. Individually, these rare parts do not reach their potential value unless you have all the rest. Additionally, the acquisition of serial number 357 and the corresponding rare parts occurred over a five-year period; during which time the collectibility of the Ford-Ferguson increased a great deal, thus driving up the value of tractor and parts.

In any case, the jobs are done and done well, and a great deal of satisfaction has accrued to those who had a hand in the work. Both Steve Williams, the new owner of the Farmall A, and Palmer Fossum, with serial number 357, will get great satisfaction out of owning these two fine old restored tractors.

*The operator's view of the restored serial number 357 Ford-Ferguson 9N. Note the nice original-type four-spoke steering wheel.*

# Clubs and Newsletters

The tractor clubs and their newsletters provide a wealth of information and lore about individual brands of antique farm tractors and equipment and have been on the scene for some time. More are springing up each year, so this list will continue to grow.

**Allis-Chalmers**
*Old Allis News*
Nan Jones, editor
10925 Love Road
Bellevue, MI 49021

**Avery**
Tru-Draft Registry
Mike Woebkenberg, editor
109 W. Center
Farmersville, OH 45325
  Includes B. F. Avery, Minneapolis-Moline/Avery, General and Wards Twin Row tractors.

**Case**
International Case Heritage Foundation
Arthur Brigham, editor
37 Harrington Drive
Bella Vista, AR 72714

J. I. Case Collectors' Association
David T. Erb, editor
Rt 2, Box 242
Vinton, OH 45686-9741
  Publishes *Old Abe's News*.

**Cockshutt**
*Golden Arrow* Magazine
John Kasmiski, editor
N7209 State Highway 67
Mayville, WI 53050
  Includes Blackhawk, Cockshutt, COOP, Farmcrest and Gambles tractors.

International Cockshutt Club
Diana Myers
2910 Essex Road
LaRue, OH 43332

**Ferguson**
Ferguson Club
George Field
Sutton House, Sutton
Tenbury Wells
Worcestershire WR15 8RJ
England

*The Ferguson Journal*
Denehurst, Rosehill Road
Stoke Heath
Market Drayden TF9 2JU
England

**Ford**
*The 9N-2N-8N Newsletter*
Gerard Rinaldi, editor
154 Blackwood Lane
Stamford, CT 06903

Fordson Tractor Club
250 Robinson Road
Cave Junction, OR 97523

**Hart-Parr and Oliver**
Hart-Parr/Oliver Collectors Club
Box 685
Charles City, IA 50616

*Oliver Collector's News*
Turtle River Toy News
Dennis Gerszewski, editor
Rt 1
Manvel, ND 58256-0044

**John Deere**
*Green Magazine*
Richard Hain, editor
RR 1
Bee, NE 68314

Two Cylinder Club
Jack Cherry
PO Box 2275
Waterloo, IA 50704

**International Harvester**
IH Collectors Association
Fremont Hoover
RR 2, Box 286
Winamac, IN 46996

*Red Power* Magazine
Daryl Miller, editor
Box 277
Battle Creek, IA 51006

**Massey-Ferguson**
*Wild Harvest* Magazine
Keith Olltrogge, editor
Box 529, 1010 S. Powell
Denver, IA 50622

**Minneapolis-Moline**
*M-M Corresponder*
Roger Mohr, editor
Rt 1, Box 153
Vail, IA 51465

*The Prairie Gold Rush Newsletter*
Roger Baumgartner, editor
Rt 1, Box 76
Walnut, IL 61376

**Rumely**
*The Rumely Newsletter*
Cass Bowyer Simpson, editor
PO Box 12
Moline, IL 61265

Rumely Registry
Ellis Welman, editor
13827 Mayfield Road
Chardon, OH 44024

**Silver King**
Silver Kings of Yesteryear
Leon Hord, editor
4520 Bullhead Road
Willard, OH 44890

**General Interest**
*Antique Power*
Patrick Ertel, editor
PO Box 838
Yellow Springs, OH 45387
    *Antique Power* is also compiling registries on Earthmaster, Friday, Leader, Sears, Sheppard and other orphan or low-production tractors.

*Belt Pulley* Magazine
PO Box 83
Nokomis, IL 62075

*Engineers & Engines*
1118 N. Raynor Avenue
Joliet, IL 60435

*Gas Engine* Magazine
PO Box 328
Lancaster, PA 17603

*Iron-Men Album*
PO Box 328
Lancaster, PA 17603

*Successful Farming*
PO Box 4536
Des Moines, IA 50336

# Repair Manuals and Books

## Repair Manuals

The *I&T Shop Service Manual*, for most popular tractor makes and models, is available from:
Intertec Publishing Corporation
PO Box 12901
Overland Park, KS 66212

These manuals are also sold by most tractor dealers and tractor parts houses. They are a must for any restorer.

Intertec Publishing Corporation is a one-hundred-year-old book and magazine publisher based in Overland Park, Kansas. Intertec's book group publishes more than 300 repair manuals for servicing farm tractors, outdoor power equipment, motorcycles, boat motors, recreational vehicles and more. The book group also publishes price guides for the agricultural, marine, outdoor power equipment, recreational vehicle, motorcycle, snowmobile and aviation industries. Their magazine group publishes numerous trade journals, newsletters, directories and more, for specialists in electrical, agricultural, horticultural, communications, engineering and automotive fields.

Bershire Implement Co. Inc.
Royal Center, IN 46978
   IHC manuals and literature

Broken Kettle Books
702 E. Madison
Fairfield, IA 52556
   Assortment of literature

Robert Campbell
RR 1, Box 348
Newberry, MI 49868

Connecticut Yankee Tractor
Ed Bezanson
85-A Dayton Road
Waterford, CT 06385
   Reprinted manuals

Jerry Erickson
RR 1
Lyle, MN 55953
   Rumely literature

Marvin Estlow
277 South Stringtown Road
Quincy, MI 49082
   Reproduction manuals for Hart-Parr models 12-24, 18-36 and 28-50

Clarence Goodburn
RR 2A-P
Madelia, MN 56062
   Catalogs, manuals and literature for all tractors

GRATCO
Tom Franklin
2384 Deborah Court
Parker, CO 80134
   Assortment of literature

*Green Magazine*
Box 11
Bee, NE 68314
   John Deere sales literature and manuals

Mike Hunchak
Box 247
Langham, Saskatchewan
Canada S0K 2I0

Jensales Co.
PO Box 985
Burnsville, MN 55337

King's Books
Box 86
Radnor, OH 43066
   Assortment of manuals

Jack Kreeger
7529 Beford Avenue
Omaha, NE 68134
   John Deere manuals for LI and L tractors

Lancaster's
Box 13636-A
Roseville, MN 55113

Lewis
RR 2, Box 508A
Yarmouth, MA 04096
   Engine catalogs, owners literature

*Massey Collector's News*
Keith Oltrogge
Box 529
Denver, IA 50622
  Photocopies of any Wallis, Massey-Harris, Massey-Ferguson or Ferguson manuals or sales catalogs

McMillan's Oliver Collectibles
9176 US Street 36
Bradford, Ohio 45308
  Oliver manuals

Medina Tractor Sales
6080 Norwalk Road
Medina, OH 44251
  Ford-Ferguson 9N repair manuals

Walter Miller
6710 Brooklawn Parkway
Syracuse, NY 13211

Glen Minarik
RR 1, Box 129
Howells, NE 68641
  International manuals and literature

Nebraska Tractor Testing Laboratory
Department of Agricultural Engineering
University of Nebraska
Lincoln, NE 68583-0832
  Copies of the complete reports of tractor tests conducted by the State of Nebraska, covering most makes and models since 1919, are available from the laboratory. Write for a list and prices.

Lee W. Pedersen
78 Taft Avenue
Lynbrook, NY 11563
  Engine literature

Mike Popp
2730 Oakhurst Lane
Franksville, WI 53126
  Massey-Harris manuals

*Red Power*
Daryl Miller
Box 277
Battle Creek, IA 51006
  International manuals and literature

Rice Equipment
20N Sheridan Road
Clarion, PA 16214
  International manuals and literature

Larry Rusch
PO Box 698
Freeport, IL 61032
  International literature

John Skarstad
Department of Special Collections
Shields Library
University of California
Davis, CA 95616
  Largest collection of shop parts manuals in the country

*9N-2N-8N Newsletter*
Gerard Rinaldi
154 Blackwood Lane
Stamford, CT 06903
  Ford 9N-2N-8N shop manuals

## Books
Books on tractors are available from:
Classic Motorbooks/Motorbooks International
PO Box 1
Osceola, WI 54020
Telephone: 800-826-6600

Recommended titles include:
  *The Allis-Chalmers Story*, by C. H. Wendel, Crestline Publishing
  *The Agricultural Tractor 1855-1950*, by R. B. Gray, Society of Agricultural Engineers
  *The American Farm Tractor*, by Randy Leffingwell, Motorbooks International. A full-color hardback history of all the great American tractor makes from John Deere to Ford with a sample of orphan makers.
  *American Gas Engines*, by C. H. Wendel, Crestline Publishing
  *Caterpillar: Great American Legend*, by Henry Rasmussen, Motorbooks International
  *Case Tractors: Steam to Diesel*, by Dave Arnold, Motorbooks International
  *Classic American Farm Gas Engines*, by Dave Arnold and C. H. Wendel, Motorbooks International
  *Classic American Farm Tractors*, by Nick Baldwin and Andrew Morland, Osprey
  *Combines*, by Bill Huxley, Osprey
  *Encyclopedia of American Farm Tractors*, by C. H. Wendel, Crestline Publishing
  *Endless Tracks in the Woods*, by James A. Young and Jerry D. Boddy, Crestline Publishing. A history of logging and crawler tractors with Holt, Best, Caterpillar, Monarch, I-H, A-C and more.
  *Ford Tractors*, by Robert N. Pripps and Andrew Morland, Motorbooks International. Full-color history of the Fordson, Ford-Ferguson N Series and the later Ford and Ferguson tractors.
  *How Johnny Popper Replaced the Horse*, by Deere & Co. Great full-color history of the John Deere General Purpose tractors.
  *International McCormick Tractors: Reliable Red*, by Henry Rasmussen, Motorbooks Interna-

tional. Full-color photo album of Farmall, Deering, McCormick, International Harvester.

*The Iron Workhorse*, by Dave Arnold and C. H. Wendel, Motorbooks International. Full-color photo album of steam tractors including Rumely, Twin City, Case and more.

*John Deere Tractors: Big Green Machines in Review*, by Henry Rasmussen, Motorbooks International

*Massey-Ferguson Tractors*, by Michael Williams, Farming Press

*Minneapolis-Moline Tractors 1870-1969*, by C. H. Wendel and Andrew Morland, Motorbooks International. Full-color history of Minne-Mo.

*Nebraska Tractor Tests*, by C. H. Wendel, Crestline Publishing

*Thoro'bred Tractors*, by Andrew Morland, Osprey

*150 Years of J. I. Case*, by C. H. Wendel, Crestline Publishing

*150 Years of International Harvester*, by C. H. Wendel, Crestline Publishing

Stemgas Publishing Company
PO Box 328
Lancaster, PA 17603

Publishes an annual directory of virtually every steam and gas-engine tractor show and threshing bee in the country

# Parts Sources

## Carburetors

Jim Alexandro
PO Box 144
Maspeth, NY 11378
  Rebuild kits

Branson Enterprises
7722 Elm Avenue
Rockford, IL 61111
  Magneto and carburetor repair

Bob Johnson
514 Brown Street
Jackson, MN 56143
  Carburetor and distributor repair

KJ Brad Repair Co.
E7577 Kennedy Road
Algoma, WI 54201
  Magneto and carburetor repair

Jack Law
RR
Pierson, IA 51048
  Magneto and carburetor repair for John Deere

## Decals

Jim Osborn Reproductions, Inc.
3070A Briarcliff Road
Atlanta, GA 30329
  General source

Surplus Tractor Parts Corp.
3215 West Main Avenue
PO Box 2125
Fargo, ND 58107
  Caterpillar, Case, Huber, Nicholas & Shepard, Silver King, Titan and Twin City

### Allis-Chalmers

Lyle Wacker
Rt 2
Osmond, NE 68765

### Cockshutt, Co-op

M. E. Brison
2731 Blacklick Eastern
Millersport, OH 43046

### Ford

M. E. Brison
2731 Blacklick Eastern
Millersport, OH 43046

Oliver Smith
305 S. 2nd Street
Denton, MD 21629
  8N decals

### Hart-Parr

Fay Orr
225 N. Pine Street
Momence, IL 60954
  12-24, 18-36 and 28-50

Frank Weber
177 4th Street
Manteno, IL 60950
  Decals for fender angle iron and transmission case

### International, McCormick-Deering

John Hiniker
1201 Lake Street
North Mankato, MN 56001

### John Deere

Travis Jorde
935 9th Avenue NE
Rochester, MN 55904

Brandon Pfieffer
7810 Upper Mt. Vernon Road
Mt. Vernon, IN 47620

### Massey-Ferguson, Wallis

Keith Oltrogge
Box 529
Denver, IA 50622

Lyle Dumont
RR 3 Box 61A
Sigourney, IA 52591

Jim Decker
103 W. Jay Street
Mankato, MN 66956
  Fender decals

**Minneapolis-Moline**
Jack Maple
Rt 1, Box 154
Rushville, IN 46173

Kenneth Funfsinn
Rt 2
Mendota, IL 61342
    Five Star decals

**Oliver**
Lyle Dumont
RR 3 Box 61A
Sigourney, IA 52591

**Rumely**
Jack Maple
Rt 1, Box 154
Rushville, IN 46173

**Emblems and Ornaments**
Knoxgun International
301 N. Cedar Street
Abington, IL 61410

Parts Duplicators
7133 Newton Street
Westminster, CO 80030

**Exhaust Manifold Dressing**
Calyx Corp.
PO Box 39277
Cincinnati, OH 45239

**Gaskets**
Gasket King Company, Ltd.
18 Hastings Avenue
Toronto, Ontario
Canada M4L 2L2

Olson's Gaskets
3059 Opdal Road E
Port Orchard, WA 98366

Wayne T. Shankle
3028 Jefferson Pike
Jefferson, MD 21755
    Gasket sets for all Deere tractors

John Weaver
PO Box 371
Middlebury, IN 46540

**Governors**
Vernon Fossum
118 Freemont Street
Northfield, MN 55057

**Magnetos**
MagElectro Service
HCR 2, Box 88
Friona, TX 79035
    Magneto, distributor, alternator, generator and starter
repair

Magneeders
Rt. 5, Box 505
Carthage, MO 64836

Mitch Malcolm
RR 1
Ottertail, MN 56571

Craig Roy
1513 Beach
Salina, KS 67401

Ed Strain
400 2nd Avenue NE
St. Petersburg, FL 33701

WJW Magnetos
Box 61
Morden, Manitoba
Canada R0G 1J0

**Paint Supplies**
DuPont
Wilmington, DE 19898

**Professional Restoration Shops**
A&B Enterprises
2189 Garrison Road
Amelia, OH 45102
    Complete restoration services

Eugene Alt
RR 2, Box 169
Audubon, IA 50025
    Complete restoration services

Richard Bockwoldt
27404 60th Avenue
Dixon, IA 52745
    Complete restoration services

Leo Brubaker
304 W. North Street
Prairie City, IA 50228

Burrell's
HCR 60, Box 8
Fairview, OK 73737
    Complete restoration services

Tom Burer
Fairfield, OH
  Complete restoration services

Jack Chandler
Rt 5, Box 505
Carthage, MO 64836
  Magneto repair and sales

Lyle Dumont
RR 3, Box 61A
Sigourney, IA 52591
  Complete restoration services

Elmer Faust
Rt 1, Box 212
Pierz, MN 56364
  Rebuilds heads, crankshafts

Russell Gibson
Box 225
Richland, MO 65556
  Complete restoration services

Jeff Graves
RR 4, Box 46
Pontiac, IL 61764
  Complete restoration services

Heartland Automotive
1612 17th Street
Central City, NE 68826
  Complete restoration services; steering wheel
restoration

JP Tools and Equipment
Tim Crawford
RR 3, Box 395
Camden, NY 13316
  Complete restoration services; specializes in engines
and drivetrains

Pat Jenuwine
21550 Irwin Street
Armada, MI 48005
  Complete restoration services

John Kasmiski
N7209 State Highway 67
Mayville, WI 53050

Mike McFarlane
1520 South Elyria Road
Wooster, OH 44691
  Complete restoration services; specializes in magneto,
distributor, and carburetor repair

Pheasant Valley Salvage
Rt 1, Box 132

Hazen, ND 58545
  Complete restoration services

Somerset Welding
Box 4055
Athens, MA 04912
  Complete restoration services

Gary Spitznogle
RR 1, Box 175A
Wapello, IA 52653

Two Cylinder Diesel Shop
Roger Marlin
RR 2, Box 241
Conway, MO 65632
  Complete restoration services; specializes in Deere
diesel tractors

Unique Wood & Metal Products
10973 Woodlawn Drive
Rochelle, IL 61068
  Machine shop and welding service, parts made and
repair

Valley View Restoration Service
Steve Bowes
RD 3, Box 319
Muncy, PA 17756
  Complete restoration services; specializes in custom
castings, sheet metal repair, shaft repair, machine shop
services

## Radiators
The Brassworks
3523 S. Higuera
San Luis Obispo, CA 93401

## Reproduction Parts
A to Z Products
PO Box 184-A
Malta, IL 60150
  Reproduction spark plugs for Deere tractors

Seth Delaney
6171 LaFayette Road
Hopkinsville, KY 42240
  Deere engines parts

Mike Green
2540 E. 29th Street
Des Moines, IA 50317
  Specializes in gas tanks, cooling tanks and other parts
of gas engines

Hinrichs Repair
Rt 2
Morrison, IL 61270
  Two-cylinder engine rings and sleeves

Hit & Miss Enterprises
Box 157
Orwell, OH 44076
　Specializes in stationary engine parts

Eugene Johnson
29 Ray Street
Cottage Hills, IL 62018
　Cork float for Schebler carburetors on Hart-Parrs and
Waterloo Boys

John Johnson
N2024 31st Road
Berlin, WI 54923
　Deere parts, old style mufflers

John Miller
Box 743
Durant, IA 52747
　Deere push-rod sleeves, water plugs

Lee W. Pedersen
78 Taft Avenue
Lynbrook, NY 11563
　Extensive list of parts including electrical supplies,
oilers and drain cocks as well as gas tank sealer

Otto Gas Engine Works
2167 Blue Ball Road
Elkton, MD 21921
　Piston rings, gaskets, carburetor kits

Paul Noake
RR 2
Rodney, Ontario
Canada N0L 2C0
　Castings for gas engines

Panning Bros. Tractor Parts
Gibson, MN 55335
　Manifolds

Ken Peterman
Rt 1, Box 61
Webster City, IA 50595
　Radiator wing caps for Oliver 70

Red Barn Shop
6770 Kelso Road
Weldon, CA 93283
　Seat backs for Deere model M; choke and start knobs
for L, LA, A and B

Rosewood Machine & Tool Co.
Duane Helman
Box 17
Rosewood, OH 43070
　Custom castings, manifolds for Oliver, Deere, Hart-
Parr, IHC and Fordson tractors

E. F. Schmidt
180 W. Kibler Street
Bluffton, OH 45817
　Cranks from belt pulley for Wallis model K and
Massey-Harris Cub Jr.

Paul Weavers Gauge
680 Sylvan Way
Bremerton, WA 98310
　Piston rings for all engines

## Sheet Metal
Ronald E. Brungart
RD 2, Box 172-A
Mill Hall, PA 17751
　Radiator parts for John Deere models L, LI and LA

Wayne Cole
Box 54
Page, ND 58064
　Allis-Chalmers A and WC

Clay Drenth
518 Buena Vista
Alta, IA 51002
　Fenders for Oliver and IHC tractors

Dave Foster
483 Schoolhouse Road
Middlebury, VT 05753
　Toolboxes for Massey-Harris models 44, 30, 33, 101,
Junior, Senior, 81 and 20

IPCO Machine
Box 35
West Mansfield, OH 43358
　Grilles for John Deere models

Kurt Kelsey
RR 2
Iowa Falls, IA 50126
　Radiator caps for Massey-Harris Challenger, Massey-
Harris oval aluminum serial number plate

Charles Krekow
RR 1, Box 14
Marcus, IA 51035
　John Deere radiator guards

Robert Lefever
879 Goshen Mill Road
Peach Bottom, PA 17563
　Large selection

George Logue, Inc.
120 S. Arch Street
Montoursville, PA 17754
　Caterpillar parts

The Louver Press
238 S. Old Orchard
Webster Grove, MO 63119
    Louvered sheet metal

Curtis Mack
RR 1, Box 156
Kenesaw, NE 68956
    Side curtains for Massey Harris 101 Super RC and
standard

Ross Implement
Harold or Jay Ross
PO Box 307
West Union, OH 45693
    John Deere parts

Bob Schreiber
1664 Stone Road
Milo, IA 50166
    Large selection

Tim Sieren
RR 2, Box 180A
Keota, IA 52248
    Radiator shutters for John Deere models A, B and G

Steiner Tractor Parts
G-10096 S. Saginaw
Holly, MI 48422
    Side shields for battery on Massey-Harris Pony

Tired Iron Farm
M. B. Holdeman
19467 County Road 8
Bristol, IA 46507

Mike J. Woebkenberg
109 W. Center
Farmersville, OH 45325
    Expanded metal grilles for Avery model R and
Minneapolis-Moline models BG and BF

Ziegenhorn & Sons, Inc.
PO Box 67
Fruitland, IA 52749
    PTO shields for Oliver and Oliver-Hart-Parr tractors

## Stainless Steel Exhaust
John Kepich Exhaust
PO Box 1365
Mentor, OH 44061

## Steering Wheels
Minn-Kota
RR 1, Box 99
Milbank, SD 57252
    Restoration and replacement steering wheels

## Tires
M. E. Miller
17386 State Highway 2
Wauseon, OH 43567
    Rare tire sizes and types, front and rear

Gempler's
Box 270-60
Mt. Horeb, WI 53572
    Rare tire sizes, tire reliners, rubber repair putty and
tire repair tools

Wallace W. Wade
Wholesale Tires
4303 C. Irving Boulevard
Dallas, TX 75247

## Tools
The Eastwood Company
580 Lancaster Avenue
Box 296
Malvern, PA 19355

Northern
PO Box 1219
Burnsville, MN 55337-0219

## Tractor Companies
Case International
700 State Street
Racine, WI 53404

Ford New Holland
500 Diller Avenue
New Holland, PA 17755

Deere and Company
John Deere Road
Moline, IL 61265

Varity Corporation
595 Bay Street
Toronto, Ontario M5G 2C3 Canada
    Massey-Harris and Massey-Ferguson

## Wheels
Madison Cast Wheel Company
PO Box 291
Fairfield, IA 52556
    Cast-iron wheels

Rick Stegbauer
5334 U.S. Highway 50
Fayetteville, OH 45118
    Rear wheel cast centers for Deere 62

## Wiring Harnesses
Y n Z's Yesterdays Parts

1615 W. Fern Avenue
Redlands, CA 92373

## New, Used and Reconditioned Parts
**Arkansas**
Bettis Tractor Parts
Crawfordsville, AR

Galen Smith
RR 4, Box 400
Bentonville, AR 72712
    Wide variety of used parts

**California**
Tri-City Tractor
12331 La Cadena
Colton, CA 92324
    Specializes in Allis-Chalmers, Caterpillar, IHC and
Ford parts

**Colorado**
Stephens Equipment
7460 E. Highway 86
Franktown, CO 80116
    Specializes in Deere parts; Deere steering wheels

**Delaware**
W. C. Littleton & Sons Inc.
Craig Littleton
PO Box 169
Laurel, DE 19956-1169

**Florida**
Ed Strain
400 2nd Avenue NE
St. Petersburg, FL 33701
    Specializes in magnetos

**Iowa**
Audubon Tractor Parts
Audubon, IA 50025

Blane Bolte
8621 180th Street
Walcott, IA 52773
    Specializes in Oliver parts

Glen N. Brink
RR 1, Box 229
Farragut, IA 51639

Central Tractor Farm & Family Center
3915 Delaware Avenue
Des Moines, IA 50313

Lloyd Creswell
406 Liston Street
Danbury, IA 51019
    Specializes in IHC TD-18 parts

Jerry Everitt & Son Tractors, Inc.
Strawberry Point, IA 52076

Iowa Falls Tractor Parts
Iowa Falls, IA 50126

David Merfeld
Box 20
Durango, IA

John Miller
Box 743
Durant, IA 52747
    Specializes in Deere models A and B parts

O'Brien County Implement
Box 156
Sheldon, IA 51201
    Specializes in Oliver parts

Robert Pollock
Vail, IA 51465
    Specializes in parts for IHC models F-20, F-12, I-9
and M

Dan Shima
409 Sheridan Drive
Eldridge, IA 52748
    Specializes in Minneapolis-Moline parts

Dennis Teubel
West Grove, IA 52538
    Specializes in Allis-Chalmers parts

Tillotson Used Parts and Equipment
Burdett Tillotson
Rt 1
Battlecreek, IA 51006

Van Noort, Inc.
Rock Valley, IA 51247

**Illinois**
Chapin Cylinder Head Co.
PO Box 259
Chapin, IL 62628-0259
    Specializes in rebuilt cylinder heads and blocks

Discount Tractor Supply
Bob Logan Jr.
Dixon and Franklin Grove, IL 61031

Doty Implement Co.
Rt 2
Princeton, IL 61356
    Specializes in Minneapolis-Moline parts

Charlie Doty
RR 2

Princeton, IL 61356
  Specializes in Minneapolis-Moline and Twin City parts

E-Jay Parts and Service
RR 1, Box 172
Gillespie, IL 62033
  New, used and rebuilt parts for 1920-1960 tractors

Gardner Sales & Service Inc.
PO Box 77
Pontiac, IL 61764

Harold Jennings
Berment, IL 61813
  Specializes in Minneapolis-Moline parts

Eugene Johnson
RR 1, Box 172
Gillespie, IL 62033

Bob Logan Tractor Co.
Box 216
Franklin Grove, IL 61031

Ray Musselman
Woodhull, IL 61490
  Specializes in Minneapolis-Moline parts

Wright's Auto & Tractor Parts
1900 N. 24th Street
Quincy, IL 62301

## Indiana
Bates Corp.
14th and Fir Road
Bourbon, IN 46504
  Specializes in IHC parts

Berkshire Implement Co. Inc.
Royal Center, IN 46978
  Specializes in IHC parts

Leesburg Tractor Parts
Leesburg, IN 46538

Don McKinsey
PO Box 94G
Wilkinson, IN 46186
  Wide assortment of spark plugs

John Weaver
PO Box 371
Middlebury, IN 46540
  Rumely head gaskets

## Kansas
Erb Repair Shop
PO Box 158
Bazine, KS 67516

James Gall
RR 1, Box 144
Reserve, KS 66643
  Specializes in parts for IHC models F-12, F-14, F-20
and F-30

Goodman Tractor Parts, Inc.
Irving Goodman
Box 1917
Wichita, KS 67201
  Specializes in rebuilt cylinder heads

John Herpick
RR 2, Box 302
Troy, KS 66087
  Specializes in Deeres and Oliver parts

Craig Roy
1513 Beach Street
Salina, KS 67401
  Specializes in Deere magnetos

Shuck's Used Parts
Rt 3
Lawrence, KS 66044
  Specializes in IHC, Minneapolis-Moline, Oliver,
Cockshutt and Deere 720 parts

## Louisiana
Wallace Gregoire Jr.
15335 Denham Road
Pride, LA 70770
  Specializes in Deere parts

Klumpp Salvage
Highway 165
Kinder, LA 70648

## Maryland
Wayne T. Shankle
3028 Jefferson Pike
Jefferson, MD 21775
  Specializes in new and used Deere parts

Starbolt Engine Supplies
3403 Buckeyestown Pike
Adamstown, MD 21710
  Specializes in gas engine parts

## Massachusetts
Townsend Equipment
Bob Smith
85 Tyler Road
Townsend, MA 01469
  Specializes in Ford parts

## Michigan
Central Michigan Tractor Parts
St. Johns, MI 48879

L. J. Goodrich
2057 Nurnberg Road
Freesoil, MI 48411
    Oliver and Case DC parts

Steiner Tractor Parts
Rt 2
Holly, MI 48442

Taylor Equipment
9356 E. 2 Mile Road
Sears, MI 49679

**Minnesota**
David Alstad
Spring Grove, MN 55974
    Specializes in IHC parts

Gene's Auto
Gene Staniszewski
Old Highway 23
Rt 1
Russell, MN 56169

Kevin Happke
RR 4, Box 9
Pierz, MN 56364
    Specializes in IHC tractors

K. Johnson
6530 Maple Grove Road
Cloquet, MN 55720
    Specializes in Deere two-cylinder tractors

Lake's Implement & Tractor Salvage
Route 7, Box 537
Brainerd, MN 56401

Mid State Tractor Parts
Rt 3
Long Prairie, MN 56347

Palmer Fossum
10201 E. 100th Street
Northfield, MN 55057
    Ford and Ferguson

Panning Bros Tractor Parts
Rt 1
Gibbon, MN 55335

TISCO
232 Lothenbach Avenue
St. Paul, MN 55118

Les Wenzel
Box 134
New Richland, MN 56072
    Specializes in Minneapolis-Moline parts

Worthington Tractor Parts
Highway 59 & 60 South
Worthington, MN 56187

**Missouri**
Austin's
Rt 4
Butler, MO 64730
    Specializes in Allis-Chalmers parts

Carburetor Shop
Eldon, MO 65026

Jack Chandler
Rt 5, Box 505
Carthage, MO 64836
    Magneto sales and repair

Mid-South Tractor Parts, Inc.
Rt 2, Box 2266
Sikeston, MO 63801

Terry Smith
RR 2, Box 49
Granger, MO 63442
    Specializes in parts for IHC tractors

Terry Smith Jr.
RR 1, Box 89
Granger, MO 63442
    Specializes in IHC parts

Welter Farm Supply
Verona, MO 65769
    Specializes in Minneapolis-Moline parts

**Mississippi**
South Central Tractor Parts
Leland, MS 38756

**Nebraska**
Glen Minarik
RR 1, Box 129
Howells, NE 68641
    Specializes in IHC parts

Tractor Supply Company
14242 C Circle Drive
Omaha, NE 68144

**New York**
Central Tractor Farm & Family Center
Box 164
Batavia, NY 14020

Lee Pederson
78 Taft Avenue
Lynbrook, NY 11563
    Specializes in gas engine parts

## North Carolina
Mid-East Tractor Parts
Goldsboro, NC 27533

## North Dakota
Brian DeWitt
RR 1, Box 132
Nazen, ND 58545
   Specializes in Deere, IHC and Minneapolis-Moline
parts

Farmers Surplus
PO Box 1765
Minot, ND 58701
   Specializes in cylinder heads

Allan Follman
Rt 1, Box 37
York, ND 58386
   Specializes in Twin City parts

Pete's Tractor Salvage, Inc.
Pete Engen
Anamoose, ND 58710

Henry Simons
665 N. 3rd Street
Carrington, ND 58421
   New, old valves, rings, gaskets and overbore kits

Surplus Tractor Parts Corp.
3215 W. Main Street
PO Box 2125
Fargo, ND 58107

## Ohio
Ed Axthelm
5071 Ashley Road
Cardington, OH 43315
   Specializes in Case and IHC parts

Dengler Tractor
6687 Shurz Road
Middletown, OH 45042

Everett Brothers
Tuscarawas, OH 44682
   Specializes in Minneapolis-Moline parts

Forest D. Glidewell
6934 State Route 121
Greenville, OH 45331
   Assorted piston rings, spark plugs, check valves

Mike McFarlane
1520 S. Elyria Road
Wooster, OH 44691
   Specializes in Deere parts

Roberts Equipment and Tractor Parts
RR 2
Camden, OH 45311

Harold Ross
Box 307
West Union, OH 45693
   Specializes in Minneapolis-Moline, Massey-Harris,
Oliver and Deere parts

Tractor Retirement Village
Edward F. Axthelm
5071 Ashley Road
Cardington, OH 43315

Vintage Tractor Parts
46178 County Road 207
Coshocton, OH 43812
   Specializes in Farmall parts

Willard Equipment Inc.
2782 State Route 99N
Willard, OH 44890

Wayne Winland
Box 114
Mantau, OH 44255
   Rubber clamps for Deere spark plugs

## Pennsylvania
Charles Burghs Machinery & Salvage
Rd 1
Harmony, PA 16037
   Specializes in tires and rims

Leaman Tractor Parts
Box 250
Willow Street, PA 17584

David Martin
RD 3, Box 392
Lewisburg, PA 17837
   Specializes in engine parts

Dean Miller
19 West Pennsylvania Avenue
Stewartstown, PA 17363
   Specializes in Dubuque-built Deere parts

Rice Equipment Co.
PO Box 687
20 N. Sheridan Road
Clarion, PA 16214-1216

Wengers Farm Machinery, Inc.
251 S. Race Street
Myerstown, PA 17067

Landis Zimmerman
1450 Diamond Station Road
Ephrata, PA 17522
   Specializes in Oliver parts

## South Dakota
ABC Company
Letcher, SD 57359
   Specializes in rebuilt heads, starters, generators,
crankshafts and radiators

Dakota Tractor Parts
Ken Steinberg
PO Box 267
Colton, SD 57018

Minn-Kota
RR 1, Box 99
Milbank, SD 57252
   Spoked steering wheels

Watertown Tractor Parts
Watertown, SD 57201

## Tennessee
Jimbo's Antique Tractor & Salvage
Rt 2
Rock Island, TN 38581

Russell Mason Tractor Co.
Winchester, TN 37398
   Specializes in Oliver parts

## Texas
Gap Tractor Salvage Inc.
Box 97
Cranfills Gap, TX 76637

MagElectro Service
HCR 2, Box 88
Friona, TX 79035
   Specializes in magnetos, distributors, alternators,
generators and starters

Glen Schueler
HCR 2, Box 88
Friona, TX 79035
   Specializes in Minneapolis-Moline parts

Tractor & Salvage Place
RR 5, Box 514
San Benito, TX 78586

## Washington
Paul Weavers Gauge
680 Sylvan Way
Bremerton, WA 98310
   Piston rings for all engines

## Wisconsin
Evansville Tractor Parts
Evansville, WI 53536

John Kasmiski
N7209 State Highway 67
Mayville, WI 53050
   Specializes in Cockshutt and Minneapolis-Moline parts

KJ Brad Repair Co.
E7577 Kennedy Road
Algoma, WI 54201
   Specializes in magnetos and carburetors

Koch Tractor Parts
RR 2, Box 0506
Richland Center, WI 53581

Madison Kipp Corp.
201 Waubesa Street
PO Box 3037
Madison, WI 53704
   Madison Kipp oiler parts used on Hart-Parr tractors

Machinery Hill, Inc.
Phillips, WI 54555

Pate Tractor and Equipment
RR 4
Baraboo, WI 53913
   Specializes in Minneapolis-Moline

Strojney Implement Co.
Mosinee, WI 54455
   Ford and Ferguson

## Canada
Brian W. Keis
33357 Townshipline Road
Rt 1
Matsqui, British Columbia
Canada V0X 1S0
   Magnetos for Allis-Chalmers and Rumely

# Safe Disposals of Parts and Chemicals

One of the real problems of doing tractor repair and restoration is what to do with the junk and poisonous fluids you inevitably generate. Everybody knows these days that two of our largest environmental problems are the related ills of landfill overuse and groundwater contamination. Unfortunately, our interest in environmental problems far outstrips our ability to find answers to them right now.

Some areas have remarkably advanced programs for disposal of hazardous waste, but most locales don't. Your first step in being a responsible garbage maker will have to be doing some of your own research. The city or county listings in your telephone blue pages will have an entry for Waste Disposal, Hazardous Waste Management or something similar. Don't expect to get many answers the first time—it can be a real trick to finally find the right outfit, since there are still no uniform rules across the country for waste management. There are, however, hazardous waste disposal sites and procedures for every location—it just may be one heck of a long way off, and your local government may not have heard about it yet. If you come across a situation like this, it'll be your ironic duty to find the answers yourself and educate your leaders.

If you strike out with the government at first, call around to local garages, body shops, and restoration specialists; they're generally forced by law to dispose of toxics in an organized manner, so they should be helpful. You may ultimately be forced to offer one of these groups some money to add your own volatiles to theirs for disposal.

The best rule of thumb as you work with chemicals and fluids is to remember that if you can smell it, it's bad news. And the stronger the odor the more dangerous it is, both to your immediate health and to the atmosphere and water table. Cleaners, paints, and all oil-derived liquids are the big things to watch out for. Dumped carelessly by the wayside, these toxic chemicals will quickly enter the water cycle and come back to haunt everybody.

The easiest solution, of course, is not to make any more of these wastes than necessary in the first place. Except for motor oil, the greatest volume of volatiles is generated by cleaning, not the actual changing of your tractor's fluids. It's best to start off with the mildest cleaners possible at first—soap and water can, in fact, do a lot of work—not just for the environment's sake but because these are also the easiest on the tractor itself.

You'll inevitably generate some hazardous materials no matter what you do, however. Things like spray cleaners and naphtha, for example—real health and environmental nightmares—are just too convenient to realistically swear off of completely. The trick is simply to catch as much of these fluids as possible after use, and to keep them tightly covered in glass or metal containers until you can safely get rid of them. Leaving pans of cleaners uncovered sends these toxins directly into the atmosphere through evaporation, so keep them covered, always.

Caked grease and ruined rags should also be kept tightly wrapped up in a cool place and disposed of along with actual fluids—they're simply volatiles that are currently trapped in solid form.

All toxics should be kept separated since cross contamination simply makes the disposal issue harder. Motor oil, for example, can actually be recycled and used as fuel for ships and other things. If it's contaminated with minute traces of brake fluid, though, the entire batch in the collection tank will be ruined.

Actual pieces of mechanical junk are generally more of a pain than a danger to dispose of. Assuming that the pieces aren't filled with fluid or particularly greasy, metal parts will sit happily inert in a landfill and actually decompose over time, albeit often a long time. If possible, you should bring big metal parts to a local junkyard; often yards will accept these pieces and use them for their scrap value. Smaller metal pieces, well, there's not much more you can do than to throw them away. The residual grease and oil won't make the local dump an ideal whooping crane nesting site, but at this point in time there aren't a lot of alternatives.

The same goes for plastic and small rubber parts, which actually do release a number of carcinogenic chemicals as they—if they—decompose. Again, though, until a coherent method of disposal is hit on, you don't have a lot of choice here but to throw them out.

Tires, on the other hand, are so well known as a dumping hazard that standards and methods for their disposal have been developed. Generally, the response has simply been to tell people that they can't dump their tires here—which ultimately is the wrong answer, since many people just get frustrated and toss them by the side of the road or in a vacant lot. A relatively recent and common development are mandatory tire buy-back laws; some areas have regulations that force tire dealers to accept used tires for disposal, usually with a small fee attached. Though there's no really good way for the dealer to get rid of the tires either, at least the problem is concentrated down to one source instead of many. Look into it.

Since regulatory agencies are currently far behind the scale of the waste problem, something else I encourage you to do is start making some noise about getting a comprehensive disposal plan developed for your city or county. Grass-roots organizations have formed in most places to look at the issue, and automotive enthusiasts need to be involved. We're the ones making a lot of the problems, so we'll need to be the ones helping to sort them out.

# Index